I0013218

Proactive Botnet Detection through Characterization Of

Distributed Denial of Service Attacks

by

Thomas S Hyslip

A Dissertation Presented in Partial Fulfillment

of the Requirements for the Degree

Doctor of Science in Information Assurance

CAPITOL COLLEGE

August 2014

© 2014 by Thomas S Hyslip
ALL RIGHTS RESERVED

Proactive Botnet Detection through Characterization Of

Distributed Denial of Service Attacks

by

Thomas S Hyslip

August 2014

Approved:

Ray A. Letteer, DSc, Chair/Mentor

Thomas M. Kromer, DSc, Committee

William A. Yurek, JD, Committee

Ebonése Olfus. DSc, Committee

Kim Schaffer, DSc, Committee

Accepted and Signed: _____ _____
                         Ray A. Letteer, DSc   Date

Accepted and Signed: _____ _____
                         Thomas M. Kromer, DSc   Date

Accepted and Signed: _____ _____
                         William A. Yurek, JD   Date

Accepted and Signed: _____ _____
                         Ebonése Olfus. DSc   Date

Accepted and Signed: _____ _____
                         Kim Schaffer, DSc   Date

_____ _____

Helen G. Barker, DM   Date
Dean, School of Business and Information Sciences
Capitol College

ABSTRACT

In this quantitative quasi-experimental study two distributed denial of service attacks were captured and the characteristics of the attacks were used to detect botnets by identifying egressing distributed denial of service attack packets at the source of the attack. A sample Dark DDoSer botnet was constructed and used to launch a distributed denial of service attack. The characteristics of the distributed denial of service attacks were used as the independent variables in a quasi-experiment where network traffic was monitored with Snort to detect DDoS packets. The dependent variable for the experiment was false positive alerts for the DDoS packets. The findings showed that the characteristics of a distributed denial of service attack can be used to pro-actively detect botnets through egress monitoring.

ACKNOWLEDGEMENTS

The completion of this dissertation and degree would not have been possible without the support of my committee members, friends, peers, and of course my family. I am very grateful to Dr. Ray Letteer for his time, support, and dedication to this endeavor. Without his leadership and guidance, this would not have been possible. I am also thankful to Dr. Tommy Kromer and Dr. Bill Yurek for their insight and assistance, as well the Capitol College faculty and staff, in particular Dr. Jason Pittman and Dr. Helen Barker.

A special thank you to my Mother, whose unwavering strength in the face of overwhelming hardship and challenge has always been the example I live by when encountering difficulty or set back. Having my own family has made me truly appreciate how much you sacrificed for Mark, Sheila, and me. Also, you bought my first Vic-20 personal computer and started me down this path.

Above all else, I am thankful to my wife Susan, who made great personal sacrifices for me during this journey. The many nights and weekends, I spent completing this dissertation and degree, left you alone to care for Reagan and maintain the house. I could not have done this without you.

TABLE OF CONTENTS

List of Tables

List of Figures

CHAPTER 1: INTRODUCTION

There has been considerable research into botnets and botnet detection techniques, but botnets are constantly evolving to stay ahead of the latest detection techniques (Dittrich, 2012). When early research on botnet detection focused on the use of passive honeypots and detection techniques aimed at detecting botnet command and control communications in centralized botnets, Botmasters began to use peer-to-peer and decentralized communications (Feily et al., 2009; Hasan, Awadi, & Belaton, 2013; Leder et al., 2009; Rossow et al., 2013; Zeng, 2012; Zhang, 2012). Botnet detection techniques were then developed to identify communications between infected computers within the decentralized botnets and Botmasters responded with the use of encrypted communications (Brezo, Santos, Bringas, & Val, 2011; Feily et al., 2009; Gu, Porras, Yegneswaran, Fong, & Lee, 2007; Zeng, 2012; Zhang, 2012). To overcome the fast changing nature of botnets, a new pro-active detection technique is required (Leder, Werner, & Martini, 2009).

This quantitative quasi-experimental study examined the feasibility of a proactive botnet detection technique whereby distributed denial of service attacks conducted by botnets are captured and the attack packets are characterized for use in egress monitoring by an intrusion detection system. The term 'botnet' is now associated with cybercrime and hacking (Awan, Disso, & Younas, 2013). However, botnets were originally designed to assist system administrators with the automated tasks of managing numerous servers (Cooke, Jahanian, & McPherson, 2005). Rossow and Dietrich (2013) considered botnets to be one of the Internet's most serious threats and Awan et al. (2013) believed botnets are a priority for many countries' cyber defenses.

This chapter provides the background of the botnet phenomenon and the research problem this dissertation explored. The research question and hypothesis used in this study are presented and the purpose of the study was examined. Finally, the research design is outlined and the conceptual framework that guided the study is provided.

Background of the Problem

Botnets were developed to assist with the administration of Internet Relay Chat (IRC) Servers (Cooke et al., 2005). IRC is an online interactive chat that allows multiple users to chat simultaneously and was created in 1988 by Jarkko Oikarinen and Darren Reed (Oikarinen & Reed, 1993). As the popularity of IRC expanded, the IRC server administrators developed software to perform automated functions to assist with the administration of the IRC Servers (Cooke et al., 2005). The computers that operated the software and performed the automated functions were referred to as robot computers and eventually as bots (Dittrich, 2012). The Eggdrop IRC bot was the first IRC Bot, developed in 1993 by Jeff Fisher to assist with the administration of IRC channels and which is still in use today (Alhomoud, Awan, Disso, & Younas, 2013; Cooke et al., 2005). Eventually, a network of bots was developed under the direction of IRC administrators and became known as a botnet (Dittrich, 2012). IRC administrators were able to send a single command from their computer and the botnet would execute that command on all the IRC Servers. Figure 1 shows a typical network configuration of an IRC botnet. Nefarious individuals realized the potential of botnets for unethical purposes and the botnets began to infect IRC users' computers without the users' knowledge and use those computers without the users' consent (Cooke et al, 2005; Cao & Qiu, 2013).

A Computer Emergency Response Team, Coordination Center (CERT/CC) advisory published on March 11, 2003, CERT/CC Advisory CA-2003-08, warned against the *GT-bot* and *sdbot* utilizing IRC to remotely control compromised systems (Householder & Danyliw, 2003). Householder and Danyliw (2003) also highlighted the growing size of botnets, with reports of *GT-bot* botnets in excess of 140,000 bots and the *sdbot* with over 7000 compromised systems. Householder and Danyliw also warned of the botnets' ability to launch distributed denial of service attacks with TDP, UDP, and ICMP packets.

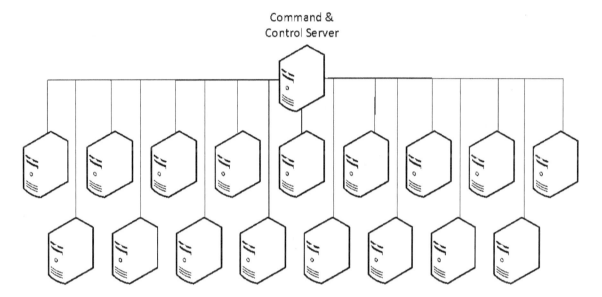

Figure 1. An IRC Botnet diagram showing the individual connections between each "bot" and the command and control server.

In December 2007, Zhuge, Holz, Han, Guo, and Zou completed a long-term study on IRC botnets. Between June 2006 and June 2007, Zhuge et al. used honeypots to collect approximately 90,000 malware samples, of which 5645 communicated with a botnet command and control server, allowing the researchers to identify 3290 unique IRC based botnets. During the study, Zhuge et al. were able to identify over 1.5 million unique bots that were functioning as part of non-obscured botnets. Of the 3290 unique botnets identified by Zhuge et al., 1904 botnets were non-obscured. Obscured botnets attempt to conceal the botnet command and control traffic by hiding the traffic as normal IRC chat (Gu, Yegneswaran, Porras, Stoll, & Lee, 2009). Gu et al. (2009) state, "By using obfuscated IRC messages (e.g., 'hello' instead of 'scan'), these botnets can evade signature-based detection and honeypot-based tracking approaches" (p. 241). Zhuge et al. (2007) observed approximately 36% of the botnets used the standard IRC communication port 6667, while the remaining botnets used a non-standard port, making the botnets harder to detect. Zhuge et al. also noted that the majority of botnet commands were related to spreading the malware to infect additional machines and performing distributed denial of service attacks. Combined, the two activities accounted for 53% of all botnet commands (Zhuge et al., 2007). The substantial use of obfuscation and non-standard IRC ports observed by Zhuge et al. are significant attempts by botnets to evade detection.

The size and scope of botnets continued to rise at an alarming rate (Hsu & Marinucci, 2013). In February 2010, Spanish authorities and the FBI dismantled the Mariposa botnet, which consisted of over 12 million compromised computers (Roscini, 2014). Only 2 years after the takedown of the Mariposa botnet, another botnet, the Metulji botnet, was dismantled by the FBI and consisted of over 20 million compromised computers (Ventre, 2013). In March 2012, Microsoft and the Financial Services Information Sharing and Analysis Center helped dismantle the family of Zeus botnets in response to over 13 million Zeus botnet infections detected worldwide (Alhomoud et al., 2013). In March 2013, the Spamhaus Project, a nonprofit organization that tracks email spam sources, was hit with a distributed denial of service attack that exceeded 300

Gigabits per second, the largest distributed denial of service attack observed to date (Fachkha, Bou-Hard, & Debbabi, 2013).

In June 2013, the Federal Bureau of Investigation, in concert with Microsoft, disrupted the Citadel botnet, which was estimated to have caused over $500 million in losses (Garber, 2013). In 2011, the overall cost of cybercrime was estimated at $114 billion annually and another $274 billion in lost time and revenue due to cybercrime (Weimer, Fry, & Forrest, 2013). Weimer et al. believe the majority of cybercrime causing almost $400 million in loses was the result of botnets.

In addition to growing in size, botnets also began to utilize decentralized methods of communications, such as peer-to-peer communications to evade detection (Feily et al., 2009; Leder et al., 2009; Raghava, Sahgal, & Chandna, 2012; Rossow et al., 2013; Zeng, 2012; Zhang, 2012). Peer-to-peer communications eliminated the need for a central command and control server and removed the single point of failure in the botnet communication structure (Ilavarasan & Muthumanickam, 2012; Lu & Brooks, 2013). With a peer-to-peer botnet, a Botmaster sends a single command to any bot and the command is passed to the other bots through peer-to-peer communications (Andriesse, Rossow, Stone-Gross, Plohmann, & Bos, 2013; Ilavarasan & Muthumanickam, 2012). Figure 2 shows a typical peer-to-peer botnet configuration.

Prior research on botnet detection has focused on the use of passive honeypots (Feily, Shahrestani, & Ramadass, 2009; Leder et al., 2009; Rossow et al., 2013). Furthermore, many botnet detection techniques attempt to detect botnet command and control communications in centralized botnets (Feily et al., 2009; Hasan, Awadi, & Belaton, 2013; Leder et al., 2009; Rossow et al., 2013; Zeng, 2012; Zhang, 2012).

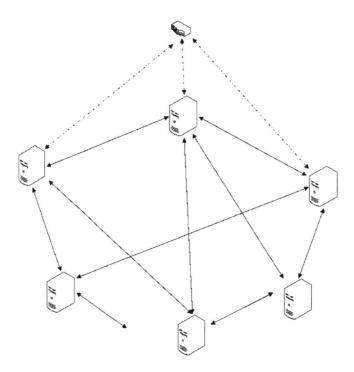

Figure 2. Peer-to-peer Botnet diagram showing the interconnection of all bots without a command and control server.

While other botnet detection techniques aimed at decentralized botnets attempt to identify communications between infected computers within the decentralized botnets (Brezo, Santos, Bringas, & Val, 2011; Feily et al., 2009; Gu, Porras, Yegneswaran, Fong, & Lee, 2007; Zeng, 2012; Zhang, 2012).

New avenues of infecting botnet computers have also been identified since 2012. In June 2012, the Blackhole exploit kit enabled botnet operators to infect new computers whenever a user visited a website configured with the Blackhole exploit kit (Li, Larsen, & van de Horst, 2013). Li, Larsen, and van de Horst (2013) warned of botnets using the Blackhole exploit kit and the use of quickly changing domain names for a webserver running the Blackhole expoit kit. By rapidly changing the domain names, Botmasters are able to avoid detection and inclusion on the known malware domain networks list (Li, Larsen, & van de Horst, 2013).

The increased use of encryption and obfuscation for botnet communications, as well as the move to decentralized botnets, limit the effectiveness of honeypots and other botnet detection techniques (Bijalwan, Thapaliyal, Pilli, & Joshi, 2013; Feily et al., 2009). This study examined the potential of a proactive botnet detection technique that characterized distributed denial of service attacks and applied egress filtering to detect outgoing distributed denial of service packets at the point of origin. By detecting the outgoing distributed denial of service attack at the source of that attack, the technique aims to identify any infected computers and help mitigate the distributed denial of service attack (Zargar, Joshi, & Tipper, 2013).

Statement of the Problem

Current botnet detection techniques are passive, and proactive measures are only taken in response to a security incident (Leder et al., 2009). Leder et al. recommended further research into pro-active botnet detection techniques to overcome the limitations of passive botnet detection techniques. Passive botnet detection techniques such as honeypots are not effective at detecting botnets which use peer-to-peer infrastructures and encrypted botnet communications (Leder et al., 2009). Furthermore, Leder et al. recommended proactive measures to counter the threat of distributed denial of service attacks carried out by botnets. This study used distributed denial of service attacks to proactively identify botnets. The specific problem addressed by this quantitative quasi-experimental study was that the vast majority of botnets now employ encrypted command

and control communications, making the use of payload signatures and honeypots

ineffective for detecting botnet communications (Rossow & Dietrick, 2013).

Purpose of the Study

The purpose of this quantitative quasi-experimental study was to show that it is

possible to proactively characterize a distributed denial of service attack and use the

characteristics to detect botnets by identifying outgoing distributed denial of service

attack packets at the source of the attack (Geva, Herzberg, & Gev, 2013; Leder et al.,

2009). By detecting the attack packets at the source of the attack, the bots participating in

the distributed denial of service attack will be identified (Zargar et al., 2013). A

quantitative quasi-experimental design was appropriate for this study because, according

to Creswell (2012), an experiment is used to determine if manipulating an independent

variable influences the outcome of the experiment or the dependent variable.

The characteristics of the distributed denial of service attack packets served as the

independent variables for this study. The independent variables for this study included

the Internet protocol, the Internet port, the TCP flags, and the flow rate of attack packets.

The dependent variable for this study was the false positive alerts for the distributed

denial of service packets as the packets egressed the local area network.

The intrusion detection system (IDS) Snort (Cisco, 2014) was used as the

instrument in this quasi-experimental study to monitor the network for distributed denial

of service attack packets. An experiment was conducted where benign internet traffic and

distributed denial of service attack packets were sent on a controlled network. The

network was monitored with Snort (Cisco, 2014) for alerts developed from the independent variables. The analysis of the research reported the results of the experiment and the statistical results of the research (Creswell, 2012).

The population sample for this study consisted of two full packet captures of distributed denial of service attacks and fifteen non-malicious packet captures of network traffic. The population and sample size are further addressed in Chapter 3. The attack packet captures were analyzed to determine the characteristics of the distributed denial of service attacks, and the characteristics were used to develop the independent variables for this study. The fifteen non-malicious packet captures were used in the experiment to test for false positive alerts of the distributed denial of service attack based on the independent variables. The experiment was performed on three identical Dell Precision 6600 computer as detailed in Appendix A.

Significance of the Study

The results of this research may be of interest to researchers and academia in the field of information assurance or cyber security, as well as network administrators and information security officers responsible for network security. Botnet detection is a heavily researched topic and botnets are rapidly changing in both communication protocols and command and control infrastructures (Cao & Qiu, 2013; Feily et al., 2009; Leder et al., 2009; Rossow & Dietrick, 2013; Wang, Wang, & Shi, 2013). Furthermore, distributed denial of service attacks are a serious concern for Internet service providers and information security professionals of nation-states (Alhomoud et al., 2013). This study contributes to both fields of study (botnet detection and distributed denial of service attacks) by developing a proactive botnet detection technique that also mitigates distributed denial of service attacks at the source of the attack.

This proactive approach is not restricted by the limitations of passive approaches, such as honeypots and network monitoring for botnet communications, by characterizing the malicious activity of the botnet and detecting the malicious activity at the source of the attack, the infected computer (Ben-Porat, Bremler-Barr, & Levy, 2013; Geva et al., 2013; Leder et al., 2009; Yang, Park & Chung, 2013). The reduction in resources is significant over current botnet detection techniques. This technique utilized only egress monitoring at the local area network level, whereas most botnet detection techniques aimed at command and control traffic monitor both egress and ingress traffic, often at the enterprise level (Brezo et al., 2011; Feily et al., 2009; Gu et al., 2007; Zeng, 2012; Zhang, 2012).

Nature of the Study

This study used a quantitative research method to investigate to what extent the independent variables affect the dependent variable. According to Creswell (2012), a quantitative research design is appropriate when the study attempts to determine if one variable affects another variable. Furthermore, Creswell suggested using an experiment when trying to establish a cause and effect relationship between an independent and dependent variable. Therefore, this study used a quasi-experimental design to measure the cause and effect relationship between the variables. A quantitative study is also appropriate when the research requires the collection of data with instruments to measure the variables in the study (Creswell, 2009). A quasi-experimental design was used for this study over a true experimental design because, according to Salkind (2012), true experiments require the random assignment of participants. This study required the use of intact groups and could not randomly assign participants; therefore, Creswell (2012) recommended the use of a quasi-experimental design.

According to Creswell (2012), when conducting an experiment if the independent variable influences the dependent variable it is permissible to say, the independent variable caused the effect, or caused the dependent variable. In this study, the experiment measured the effect on the dependent variable, i.e., the number of false positive detections by the intrusion detection system. The experiment tested each independent variable separately to determine the independent variable's effect on the number of false positives detections. The experiment also tested combinations of independent variables to determine the effect on the number of false positive detections for each combination. Table 1 shows the order of tests that were used for the experiment and the independent variables that were tested separately and together.

Table 1
Order of Experimental Tests

Number of Independent Variables	Snort Rule
1	**Protocol**, Internal IP, any -> External IP, any, none, none
2	**Protocol**, Internal IP, any -> External IP, **Port**, none, none
2	**Protocol**, Internal IP, any -> External IP, any, **flags**, none
2	**Protocol**, Internal IP, any -> External IP, any, none, **rate**
3	**Protocol**, Internal IP, any -> External IP, **Port, flags**, none
3	**Protocol**, Internal IP, any -> External IP, **Port**, none, **rate**
3	**Protocol**, Internal IP, any -> External IP, any, **flags, rate**
4	**Protocol**, Internal IP, any -> External IP, **Port, flags, rate**

Note. The elements in bold are the independent variables being used for each test.

The goal of the study was to manipulate the independent variables and reduce the number of false positive Snort alerts. This study used a quantitative quasi-experimental design to detect botnets through the use of independent variables developed from distributed denial of service attack characteristics. The independent variables of this study included the Internet protocol, Internet port, the TCP flags, and the flow rate of attack packets.

The results of the experiment were analyzed and interpreted with descriptive and inferential statistical formulas. The descriptive statistics included the mean, mode, and median, as well as the variance, standard deviation and range for the experiment results. The inferential statistics included the Student's paired t-test and the repeated measures analysis of variance between groups, ANOVA test. The paired t-test was used to compare the results of the experiment when utilizing one, two, three, or four independent variables. The repeated measures ANOVA test was used to interpret the results of all four groups together.

A quantitative research design was chosen for this study rather than a qualitative or mixed methods design because the study used instruments and collected numeric data to explain the relationship between known variables (Creswell, 2012). According to Creswell, qualitative research designs are used to understand and explore the central phenomenon of a problem. Qualitative designs also collect data through interviews and questionnaires to analyze participant's answers (Creswell, 2012). A mixed method research design is used when the use of both quantitative and qualitative research provide a better understanding of the research problem (Creswell & Plano Clark, 2011). A mixed method research design is also appropriate when the initial research results require further explanation (Creswell, 2009). For this study, neither qualitative nor mixed method research provided insight into the characteristics of distributed denial of service attacks to detect the location of botnets, hence, the choice of a quantitative quasi-experimental research design for this study (Creswell, 2012).

Research Question and Hypothesis

According to Creswell (2012), research questions narrow the purpose statement and relate the variables. The research question for the study was: to what extent can the characteristics of a distributed denial of service attack (the Internet protocol, the Internet port, the TCP flags, and the flow rate of attack packets) be used to pro-actively detect botnets? This question was investigated using a full network packet capture of a distributed denial of service attack to develop characteristics of the distributed denial of service attack. The characteristics were then be used to detect the botnet that executed the distributed denial of service attack. According to Creswell (2009), independent variables are variables that affect outcomes or influence other variables. For this study, the characteristics of the distributed denial of service attack served as the independent variables. The independent variables were the Internet protocol, the Internet port, the TCP flags, and the flow rate of attack packets. Creswell (2009) defined a dependent variable as the outcome in quasi-experimental research. The dependent variable for this study was the number of false positive alerts for distributed denial of service attack packets as the packets egressed the local area network.

Similar to research questions, hypothesis narrow quantitative purpose statements, but also provide a prediction about the outcome of the research (Creswell, 2012). Creswell and Plano Clark (2011) stated that if past research indicates there will be a relationship among the variables, a quantitative hypothesis is usually developed for a study. For this study, the hypothesis states the characteristics of distributed denial of service attacks (the Internet protocol, the Internet port, the TCP flags, and the flow rate of attack packets) can be used to reduce the number false positive alerts for distributed denial of service attack packets. This hypothesis was used to guide the research for this study to determine if a relationship existed between the variables.

In contrast to a hypothesis, Creswell (2012) defined a null hypothesis as a prediction that there is no relationship between variables. The null hypothesis for this study states that The null hypothesis for this study states that the characteristics of distributed denial of service attacks (the Internet protocol, the Internet port, the TCP flags, and the flow rate of attack packets) cannot be used to reduce false positive alerts for distributed denial of service attack packets while detecting botnets that participate in the distributed denial of service attack.

Conceptual Framework

Since the methodology for this study is based on egress monitoring by intrusion detection systems, its conceptual framework is based on the National Institute of Standards and Technology (NIST), Special Publication 800-94, Revision 1 (Draft) (Scarfone & Mell, 2012), titled, "Guide to Intrusion Detection and Prevention Systems." There is a vast amount of research on the use of intrusion detection systems for botnet detection; however, that research is focused on the detection of command and control communications and full packet inspection (Brezo et al., 2011; Feily et al., 2009; Garant & Lu, 2013; Gu et al., 2007; Gu et al., 2009; Gu, Zhang, & Lee, 2008; Paxton, Ahn, & Shehab, 2011; Rossow & Dietrich, 2013; Rossow et al., 2013; Zeng, 2012; Zhang, 2012).

The concepts used by Gu et al. (2007), Gu, Zhang, et al. (2008), and Garant and Lu (2013) for detecting botnet command and control communications with intrusion detection systems provide a foundation for detecting botnets with distributed denial of service attacks. Gu et al. (2007) used Snort (Cisco, 2014) to monitor Internet ports typically used by botnets for scanning activity, payload inspection for executable downloads, and also developed 246 Snort rules for command and control communications based on protocol, behavior and payload signatures. Garant and Lu (2013) developed a signature for botnet communications using six features of network traffic: 1. flow length in bytes, 2. flow packet count, 3. flow protocol, 4. flow duration, 5. flow direction, and 6. TCP flags. Gu, Zhang et al. (2008) used network flow data for TCP and UDP flows to cluster possible botnet communications and analyze the correlations for botnet detection. Gu, Zhang et al. (2008) used the IP address and port for both the source and destination, as well as the time and duration for each communication, and the number of number of packets and bytes to identify flow records of possible botnet communications.

In NIST Special Publication 800-94, Scarfone and Mell (2012) detailed three detection methodologies for intrusion detection and prevention systems: anomaly-based detection, stateful protocol analysis, and signature-based detection. Scarfone and Mell defined signature based detection as the practice of comparing signatures with network traffic to detect security events. Scarfone and Mell provided examples of the word root within a packet or an attachment to an email with an .exe file. Anomaly-based detection relies on learned normal network activity and alerts administrators to network activity that is outside normal activity, such as a significant increase in network bandwidth

(Scarfone and Mell, 2012). Lastly, Scarfone and Mell explained stateful protocol analysis as identifying commands, protocols, or network activity that are out of sequence or other uses not defined in the rules of the intrusion detection and prevention system.

The method for this study utilized a signature-based detection based on the header data of captured distributed denial of service attack packets. The signature was developed based on the characteristics of the attack packets. The characteristics included the Internet protocol, the Internet port, the TCP flags, and the flow rate of the attack packets. Snort (Cisco, 2014) intrusion detection system rules were then written based on the characteristics and used for egress monitoring for attack packets. Those characteristics served as the independent variables for this quantitative quasi-experimental study.

Definition of Terms

The following terms are used throughout this dissertation and are defined for this study:

Botmaster: An individual in control of a botnet that issues commands, updates, and utilizes the botnet for criminal activity (Liao, Li, Yang, Chen, Tsai, & Chang, 2012).

Botnet: A network of compromised computers, which are controlled by an administrator through common Internet communication protocols, including Internet Relay Chat (IRC), Peer-to-Peer (P2P), and Hypertext Transfer Protocol (HTTP) (Wang & Yu, 2009).

Distributed denial of service attack (DDOS): An attack consisting of many compromised computers, often in the thousands, initiating simultaneous connections to a target computer in an attempt to overwhelm the available resources of the computer and render the computer non-responsive to legitimate connections (Tsai, Chang, & Ming-Szu, 2010).

Internet Control Message Protocol (ICMP): A control protocol that is part of the TCP/IP protocol suite and is used to test the status of networks and report errors. It does not carry any application data (Trost, 2010)

Internet Protocol (IP): The packet-switching protocol for the Internet layer of the TCP/IP protocol suite, which uses logical addressing to route packets on the Internet (Trost, 2010)

Intrusion Detection System (IDS): A computer system that monitors network traffic for suspicious or malicious activity and alerts system administrators of possible rules violations for network activity (Whitman & Mattord, 2012).

Intrusion Prevention System (IPS): A computer system that monitors network traffic for suspicious or malicious activity and alerts system administrators of possible rules violations for network activity and also attempts to prevent the malicious activity (Whitman & Mattord, 2012).

Malware: Is a term formed by merging the words malicious and software and is collectively used to refer to any software that is installed on a computer without the user's consent or beyond the user's knowledge (V.P., Laxmi, & Gaur, 2009).

Transmission Control Protocol (TCP): The standard transport layer protocol for the Internet and is responsible for sequencing, segment assembly, and error recovery in connection based communications (Trost, 2010).

User Datagram Protocol (UDP): The standard connectionless transport layer protocol for Internet traffic that does not maintain a connection and require error checking (Trost, 2010).

Assumptions

For this study, it was assumed that botnets use the same attack characteristics for repeat attacks. Current research supported the assumption that botnets will use the same attack characteristics for repeat attacks (Gu, Perdisci, Zhang, & Lee, 2008; Hussain, Heidemann, & Papadopoulos, 2006). Hussain et al.'s (2006) research showed repeat distributed denial of service attacks can be attributed to the same botnet because the same computer equipment and malware are used to conduct the distributed denial of service attacks. Gu, Perdisci et al. (2008) concluded members of a botnet conduct the same or similar activities at the same, such as receiving commands or executing malicious activities, and researchers are able to cluster like activity to detect botnets.

Scope and Limitations

The nature of the study calls for a pro-active approach to detecting botnets and relies on the purchasing of a distributed denial of service attack from a Botmaster advertising attacks for sale at online forums. For purposes of this study, a previously captured distributed denial of service attack was used. The ethical concerns of paying a criminal Botmaster to launch a distributed denial of service attack using compromised computers that make up a botnet outweigh the benefit of capturing a live attack. Therefore, the previously captured distributed denial of service attack was used for this study.

The previously captured distributed denial of service attack used for this study consisted of a SYN flood distributed denial of service attack that was executed by a variant of the *Black Energy* botnet. The *Black Energy* Botnet was a popular botnet between 2008 and 2010 that had many distributed denial of service attack features (Shah, 2011).

Furthermore, a *Dark DDoser* botnet was established in a controlled virtual environment and used to launch a SYN flood distributed denial of service attack. The attack was captured and used in conjunction with the *Black Energy* botnet attack for this study. Therefore, the scope of this study was limited to SYN flood distributed denial of service attacks.

The results of this study may be generalized to all botnets that use SYN flood distributed denial of service attacks. A SYN flood distributed denial of service attack is effective against any computer or server using the transmission control protocol (TCP) for transport layer internet communications (Ben-Porat, Bremler-Barr, & Levy, 2013). A SYN flood attack targets the three-step communication process of the TCP communications by overwhelming a computer with excessive SYN requests (Ben-Porat et al., 2013).

Delimitations

Cottrell and McKenzie (2010) defined delimitations as constraints or restrictions the researcher placed on a study. This study was not conducted to detect botnets that execute reflective distributed denial of service attacks, nor DNS amplification distributed denial of service attacks since both attacks involve the use of third party computers or DNS servers to send the actual attack packets to the victim computer (Kline, Beaumont-

Gay, Mirkovic, & Reiher, 2009; Meenakshi, Raghavan, & Bhaskar, 2011). This research focused on botnets that execute SYN flood distributed denial of service attacks directly from the botnet to the targeted victim system.

Summary

Botnets have evolved to become one of the most serious threats to the Internet and there is substantial research on both botnets and botnet detection (Alhomoud et al., 2013; Rossow &Dietrich, 2013). However, past research has focused on the use of passive honeypots for botnet detection (Feily et al., 2009; Leder et al., 2009; Rossow et al., 2013) and on detecting botnet command and control communications (Brezo et al., 2011; Feily et al., 2009; Gu et al., 2007; Zeng, 2012; Zhang, 2012). The significance of this study is the pro-active approach of characterizing distributed denial of service attacks and implementing egress monitoring to detect botnets when the botnets conduct future distributed denial of service attacks (Ben-Porat et al., 2013; Geva et al., 2013; Leder et al., 2009; Yang et al., 2013).

The nature of this study is quantitative and a quasi-experimental research design was used. The research investigated whether characteristics of denial of service attacks, the Internet protocol, the Internet port, the TCP flags, and the flow rate of attack packets can be used to detect distributed denial of service attacks through egress monitoring at the source of the attack while reducing false positive detections. The distributed denial of service attack characteristics, the Internet protocol, the Internet port, the TCP flags, and the flow rate of attack packets served as the independent variables for the quantitative research. The dependent variable was the false positive detections of distributed denial of service attack packets as the packets egress the local area network.

The literature review in Chapter 2 provides a chronological review of the evolution of botnets and botnet detection techniques. The review also covers distributed denial of service attacks because botnets are the underlying infrastructure that enable distributed denial of service attacks and botnets and distributed denial of service attacks are inherently linked (Zargar et al., 2013) Chapter 2 concludes with the current research of botnets and botnet detection techniques.

CHAPTER 2: LITERATURE REVIEW

According to Creswell (2012) a literature review justifies the proposed research problem and defines how one's research will increase the knowledge of the field. A literature review is also necessary to ensure the research question has not already been answered (Snieder & Larner, 2009). The literature reviewed for this study was drawn from numerous databases including: ProQuest, IEEE Computer Society Digital Library, Google Scholar, and the IEEE Xplore Digital Library. The keywords used in the search included *botnet, distributed denial of service, malware, denial of service, botnet detection, botnet identification, and proactive botnet.* The chronological literature review examined the history and evolution of botnet detection as botnets changed from a centralized command and control structure to a decentralized peer-to-peer control structure, and the ability to detect distributed denial of service attacks conducted by botnets. The review showed traditional botnet detection techniques rely on passive techniques, primarily honeypots, and that honeypots are not effective at detecting peer-to-peer and other decentralized botnets (Feily et al., 2009; Leder et al., 2009; Rossow et al., 2013; Zeng, 2012; Zhang, 2012). Furthermore, the detection techniques aimed at decentralized and peer-to-peer botnets focus on detecting communications between the infected bots (Fedynyshyn, Chuah, & Tan, 2011; Feily et al., 2009; Ilavarasan & Muthumanickam, 2012; Leder et al., 2009; Zeng, 2012; Zhang, 2012). Lastly, the literature reviewed showed the vast majority of botnet detection techniques attempt to identify communications between the command and control server and the botnet (Brezo et al., 2011; Feily et al., 2009; Gu et al., 2007; Zeng, 2012; Zhang, 2012). While observing command and control traffic has been an effective detection technique to date,

Dittrich (2012) suggested that passive monitoring for command and control traffic will become less effective as botnets employ random topology and increase the use of encryption and obfuscation.

History of Botnet Detection

The Honeynet project was a pioneer in botnet detection (Feily et al., 2009). The Honeynet project began in 1999 as an information mailing list for information security professionals and was established as a non-profit information security research organization with the mission to learn about computer and network attacks in 2000 (Spitzner, 2003). Spitzner (2003) defined a honeynet as a network of computers placed on the Internet with the intention of capturing unauthorized activity directed at the computers. The purpose of a honeynet is to monitor network activity after malicious software is installed on the honeynet's computers and learn how the malicious software operates, with the goal of capturing new and unknown attacks and malicious software (Spitzner, 2003). In a 2009 survey of botnet detection techniques, Feily et al. (2009) found a vast majority of the botnet detection techniques rely heavily on honeynets because honeynets are simple to operate and are passive to the botnet, so no interaction is required with the botmaster or command and control server by the researcher. The honeynet receives the instructions or commands from the botnet operator but does not itself respond or execute the commands (Spitzner, 2003).

In July 2005, Cooke et al. proposed monitoring transmission control protocol (TCP) port 6667 on live networks for IRC botnet command and control traffic as a possible botnet detection technique. TCP port 6667 is the default IRC port, but Cooke et al. recognized the default port is easily changed to non-standard ports, so the detection technique of monitoring networks for IRC traffic on TCP 6667 was not recommended. Cooke et al. proposed a second botnet detection technique utilizing a honeypot and capturing traffic between the honeypot and the IRC botnet command and control server. The captured traffic was then analyzed to develop signatures of botnet traffic (Cooke et al, 2005). Cooke et al. determined there were no connection-based variables that would be useful in detecting botnets via monitoring network traffic for command and control traffic. The botnets' ability to modify the mode or behavior of communications can easily defeat detection techniques based on command and control traffic analysis (Cooke et al., 2005).

In 2007, Gu et al. developed BotHunter, a detection technique focused on detecting inbound command and control traffic with bots inside a local area network and outbound traffic that conducts scans of external IP addresses. Gu et al. developed BotHunter as two plugins and one ruleset for the open source, intrusion detection system, Snort (Cisco, 2014). For inbound traffic detection, Gu et al. (2007) developed the Snort plugin, Statistical Scan Anomaly Detection (SCADE) which monitors 24 TCP and 4 UDP inbound ports for possible command and control traffic associated with botnet malware. SCADE also monitors outbound traffic for hosts that scan a large number of external IP addresses or have high number of failed external connections. The egress monitoring of outbound traffic by SCADE is relative to this study; however, SCADE does not monitor for malicious distributed denial of service attack packets as suggested for this study.

The second Snort (Cisco, 2014) plugin developed by Gu et al. Statistical Payload Anomaly Detection Engine (SLADE) attempts to detect malicious payloads through packet inspection of all inbound traffic. SLADE utilizes anomaly detection to determine if payloads are suspicious based on the payloads standard deviation from test payloads of normal Internet traffic (Gu et al., 2007). The problem with deep packet inspection is the large overhead associated with inspecting voluminous amounts of traffic in large networks (Zhang, 2012). Gu et al. (2007) also developed four rulesets for Snort (Cisco, 2014) to monitor 1383 heuristics of known botnets and malware. BotHunter's final phase of detection is a correlation matrix, that weighs each Snort alert and applies a coefficient based on the type of alert to determine if a host is infected (Gu et al., 2007). SLADE's detection of malicious payloads is also relevant to this study, but SLADE does not detect outbound traffic.

Gu, Zhang, and Lee (2008) built upon BotHunter to develop BotSniffer, a system designed to detect botnet command and control traffic through anomaly detection. BotSniffer is limited to detecting IRC and HTTP botnets that use a centralized command and control server, but no prior knowledge of a botnet's signature is required to detect hosts within a local area network (Gu, Zhang, et al., 2008). In both IRC and HTTP botnets, Gu, Zhang, et al. recognized that the bots must make connections to the command and control server to obtain commands and then the bots will have similar activity based on the commands. Based on research conducted by Zhuge et al. (2007), Gu and his associates developed BotSniffer to recognize similar behavior by hosts after communicating with a possible command and control server located at the same IP address. Zhuge et al. (2007) had determined that over 28% IRC botnet commands are for spreading malware and 25% of IRC commands are for distributed denial of service attacks. Based on these statistics, Gu, Zhang et al. (2008) developed anomaly based algorithms to detect command and control traffic, as well as network scanning, with the open source intrusion detection system, Snort (Cisco, 2014). Utilizing previously captured network traffic with known botnet infections, Gu, Zhang et al. (2008) successfully tested BotSniffer and detected 100% of IRC botnet command and control traffic with a false positive rate of 0.16%.

Challenges and Issues in Botnet Detection

Feily et al. (2009) conducted a survey of botnet detection techniques and classified them into four categories: anomaly-based, signature-based, DNS-based, and mining-based. The four techniques are considered passive detection techniques and rely on monitoring and analysis of network traffic. Specifically, Feily et al. stated signature-based detection techniques are only effective against known botnets and require rules aimed at known botnets for intrusion detection systems (IDS). The signature-based techniques will only identify infected hosts located behind the IDS and possibly the IP address of the computer communicating with an infected host (Feily et al., 2009).

According to Feily et al. (2009), anomaly-based detection techniques detect malicious behavior in a network based on network traffic abnormalities; however, anomaly-based techniques are able to overcome the issues of identifying previously unidentified botnets, but they can be defeated if botnets mimic normal network traffic. Research by Karasaridis, Rexford, and Hoeflin (2007) in anomaly-based detection techniques demonstrated the ability to calculate the size of botnets and identify command and control servers by analyzing flow data from the transport layer in large scale networks. However, this technique was only tested against IRC based botnets utilizing a centralized command and control server (Karasaridis et al., 2007). Karasaridis et al.

recommended additional research in the detection of peer-to-peer and HTTP based botnets.

Domain Name System (DNS)-based detection techniques are effective against centralized command and controller botnets that rely on DNS for communication between the botnet command and control server and the infected computers (Feily et al, 2009). Feily et al. detailed many DNS-based techniques for identifying botnet command and control servers and command and control traffic, but none are effective against peer-to-peer botnets that are decentralized and do not use command and control servers.

Feily et al. (2009) also surveyed mining-based detection techniques aimed at identifying command and control traffic between command and control servers and the botnet. Feily et al. define mining-based detection as analyzing network traffic for botnet command and control traffic using machine learning, classification or clustering of similar traffic. All but one of the mining-based detection techniques surveyed by Feily et al. were focused solely on IRC based botnets and not effective against peer-to-peer botnets; furthermore, Field et al. (2009) stated botnet command and control traffic is hard to identify because botnets use standard network protocols for command and control communications. BotMiner is a network anomaly-based detection system for botnets within a local area network and was the only detection technique effective against IRC, HTTP and peer-to-peer botnets (Feily et al, 2008).

Gu, Perdisci et al. (2008) developed BotMiner as a general botnet detection technique that is effective against any botnet command and control protocol or structure; in addition, BotMiner was designed to function without any prior intelligence of botnet protocols or signatures. BotMiner detects botnets by clustering hosts based on similar traffic and malicious activities (Gu, Perdisci et al., 2008). Gu, Perdisci et al.'s research focused on the botnet communications since botnets much communicate with a command and control server of with other bots to receive commands such as when to scan or launch attacks. In order for the bots to function as a botnet, the bots must receive the same commands; therefore the researchers believed the same botnet would have similar traffic and malicious activities (Gu, Perdisci et al., 2008). Based on the similar traffic and activities, BotMiner clusters similar communication traffic into C-plane traffic and like malicious activities into A-plane traffic (Gu, Perdisci et al., 2008). Gu, Perdisci et al. then detected botnets by correlating the A-plane and C-plane traffic.

To cluster communications within the C-plane traffic, Gu, Perdisci, et al. (2008) monitored TCP and UDP network flow data and recorded IP addresses, network ports time and duration of the traffic, and the number of packets and bytes transferred in each direction. Gu, Perdisci et al. used Snort (Cisco, 2014) to capture A-plane traffic based on malicious activities, scanning, spam, and binary downloads. The C-plane clusters were then cross-correlated with the A-plane clusters to identify hosts that are part of a botnet (Gu, Perdisci et al., 2008).

Feily et al. (2009) concluded the majority of botnet detection techniques only work against specific command- and control-based botnets and are ineffective against botnets that update their command and control protocols to peer-to-peer, or other decentralized communications. Therefore, future detection techniques should be based on DNS traffic and network anomalies, such as BotMiner (Feily et al., 2009).

Wang and Yu (2009) developed a botnet detection technique aimed at detecting command and control communications of botnets, irrespective of the particular botnet.

Wang and Yu based the detection technique on the timing and uniformity of botnet communications; Wang and Yu's technique used only the packet size and timing interval between arriving packets as variables to determine if network traffic was botnet command and control communications. Experimental results showed the technique to be effective for detecting command and control traffic of four different botnet types. However, the technique is only effective against botnets with a centralized command and control structure (Wang & Yu, 2009).

Nagaraja, Mittal, Hong, Caesar and Borisov (2010) developed BotGrep, a botnet detection technique focused on peer-to-peer botnets that use structured overlay networks for communication. Nagaraja et al. developed an algorithm that isolates peer-to-peer communication based on the pairing of nodes that communicate with each other. BotGrep then utilizes graph analysis to identify botnet hosts. Although BotGrep is not affected by botnets that vary ports or use encryption, BotGrep does require a seeding of botnet information to be effective; therefore, the researchers recommend operating a honeynet to capture botnet intelligence that can be used by BotGrep to identify the rest of the botnet (Nagaraja et al., 2010).

In June 2010, Wang, Sparks and Zou designed an advanced hybrid peer-to-peer botnet to highlight the emerging threat of peer-to-peer botnets and advanced features that botmasters may incorporate into botnets in the future. Wang et al. (2010) reviewed previous research into detecting botnets and concluded previous botnet research had focused on the command and control server of the botnet. Prior to peer-to-peer botnets, the majority of botnets communicated via IRC or HTTP and relied upon command and control servers to communicate with the botnet; therefore, the researchers saw the command and control server as the weak point in the botnet and focused on techniques to disable them (Wang et al., 2010). Wang et al. explained that new communication techniques such as peer-to-peer will enable criminals to communicate with botnets without a central command and control server; thus, new research is needed into how to detect and shut down peer-to-peer botnets.

Wang et al. (2010) designed an advanced peer-to-peer botnet that has no bootstrap procedures with each bot only having a limited peer list for the botnet. Based on these features, Wang et al. believed it would be very difficult to detect the botnet unless the botnet is discovered before the botmaster issues the first update command to the botnet. By detecting the infection early, the bots would not receive the updated peer list and the bots would not be able to communicate. Wang et al. recommended the continued use of honeypots to detect and shutdown botnets; if a honeypot is infected by a new botnet, researchers would be able to quickly identify the peer list and shutdown the botnet.

Lee, Kwon, Shin and Lee (2010) developed a botnet detection technique that analyzed DNS traffic generated by botnets to identify domain names of botnet command and control servers. Lee et al. believed that botnets would make repeated queries of the same DNS names so a statistical pattern could be developed to identify the bots making the queries; Lee et al. also thought that the DNS traffic could be analyzed to identify new flux domain names that have not been used by the botnet. To test their technique, Lee et al. captured DNS traffic on a live network for two weeks and were able to identify botnet DNS queries and new fast flux domains for botnets. To explore the DNS traffic, the researchers used statistics and graph structure analysis to identify DNS queries that were possible botnet command and control server domains. Lee et al. stated that DNS analysis techniques are not effective against peer-to-peer botnets but believed they may be incorporated with other techniques that are effective against peer-to-peer botnets.

Zeng, Hu and Shin (2010) developed a botnet detection technique that incorporates both host level detection and network level detection. Zeng et al. believed that by combining the host and network level detections and correlating the alerts, their technique would increase the rate of detection and overcome the limitation of each technique alone. Zeng et al. used registry changes, file system modifications and network stack changes to alert for possible botnet malware activity on host detections and utilized netflow data for network level detection but avoided full packet inspection, which ensures privacy for network users. The researchers successfully tested their combined host and network detection technique and believe this is the first combined host and network level detection technique developed. Zeng et al. stated that their combined host detection technique was effective against IRC, peer-to-peer, and HTTP botnets, but noted that the technique is limited by the scalability. Zeng et al. recognized that the host level detection technique requires installation on all hosts within an organization and may only be accomplished in enterprise networks.

Brezo et al. (2011) also surveyed the available research in botnet detection techniques and concluded IRC is still the main protocol for command and control communications of botnets. Brezo et al. highlighted the use of IRC by Anonymous to coordinate and launch distributed denial of service attacks in 2011. Brezo et al. believed botnet detection techniques should focus on IRC channels, but detection techniques should also consider peer-to-peer messaging and communication through HTML pages as forms of botnet command and control communication.

Paxton, Ahn and Shehab (2011) created a computer system called MasterBlaster which they used to monitor botnets by purposely infecting the system with a known botnet and then capturing the traffic to the infected bot. Paxton et al. were able to successfully infect MasterBlaster with an IRC shellbot type botnet and observe the commands issued by numerous botmasters. Based on the different commands and attacks patterns, Paxton et al. identified 10 unique botmasters and observed the botmaster's commands and targets.

Paxton et al. (2011) explained that, often, numerous individuals use the same botnet and there has been little to no research into the actual botmasters that use the botnet. Paxton et al. noted the botnet is just a tool for the botmaster and more research needs to focus on the actual users of the botnets. Paxton et al. were able to successfully infect MasterBlaster with an IRC shellbot type botnet and observe the behavior for one month; their analysis revealed 10 different botmasters used the botnet with one botmaster issuing over 90% of the commands. Paxton et al. used the social behavior of people and the reflective-impulsive model to determine when a different botmaster is using the botnet and which commands correspond to which botmaster. Paxton et al. observed that, to further identify individual botmasters, additional study of peer-to-peer botnets with the ability to decrypt command and control communications is necessary.

Distributed Denial of Service Attacks

Distributed denial of service attacks are a major threat to the Internet, and botnets are the reason attackers are able to conduct distributed denial of service attacks (Zargar et al, 2013). Zargar et al. noted that research into distributed denial of service attack prevention, detection, response and mitigation is inherently linked to botnet detection because the botnet is the underlying infrastructure that enables the distributed denial of service attack. To effectively counter a distributed denial of service attack, the perpetrating botnet must be identified and the distributed denial of service attack countered as close to the botnet source as possible (Zargar et al., 2013). Therefore, the research into distributed denial of service attacks was reviewed for relevant material related to botnet detection.

Hussain et al. (2006) developed a technique for fingerprinting distributed denial of service attacks to determine if subsequent distributed denial of service attacks were perpetrated by the same attack tool and botnet computers. Hussain et al. based the fingerprinting of distributed denial of service attacks on spectral characteristics of the distributed denial of service attack. Specifically, Hussain et al. showed that the attack tool and the computer's specifications define attack packet streams and using the frequency spectra of the attacks, those attacks can be fingerprinted for comparison. Hussain et al. believed the fingerprinting of distributed denial of service attacks can aid in attribution for attacks. Hussain et al. tested the fingerprints of attacks by capturing attacks at an Internet Service Provider and analyzed the attack packets to determine if the attack was executed by the same botnet. Hussain et al. did not attempt real time fingerprinting and detection, as all of their research was conducted on packet captures.

In 2008, Yi, Yu, Zhou, Hai and Bonti developed a filtering scheme to detect distributed denial of service attacks utilizing spoofed IP addresses and filter the distributed denial of service traffic at the victim site based on hop counts to the source IP address. Yi et al. used the geographic location of IP address schemes and the time to live (TTL) values of packets to build a normal hop count for packets from different geographic locations during normal Internet traffic; spoofed distributed denial of service packets will fall outside the normal hop count and be filtered out.

Khattak, Bano, Hussain and Anwar (2011) recognized the increased size of network logs during distributed denial of service attacks and the problems associated with reviewing the large network logs to identify victim computers and the distributed denial of the service attacker's location. Khattak et al. used MapReduce (Dean & Ghemawat, 2004) to forensically analyze large data sets of network traffic to identify distributed denial of service traffic. MapReduce utilizes distributed processing across a cluster of computers to analyze network logs (Dean & Ghemawat, 2004). Khattak et al. (2011) used network logs provided by Lincoln Laboratory (2014), which were previously analyzed for distributed denial of service traffic by that organization. By utilizing these logs, Khattak et al. were able to compare the results of the distributed denial of service detection utilizing MapReduce to Lincoln Labs' results. Utilizing MapReduce, Khattak et al. saw a significant decrease in time to identify malicious traffic and infected computers. Khattak et al. also realized significant time savings as the size of the network logs increased. Prior to analyzing the network traffic, Khattak et al. had to convert packet capture (pcap) files to text files because MapReduce can only accept text files; the additional time to convert the files actually increased the overall time to analysis the network traffic. Khattak et al. recommended developing a binary convertor to work in conjunction with MapReduce so pcap files can be used with MapReduce.

Jun, Oh and Kim (2011) developed a distributed denial of service detection technique utilizing four entropy thresholds which were based on volume traffic, destination IP addresses, source port, and packet creation rate. Jun et al. tested the four entropy thresholds in numerical order, i.e., if the first threshold was met, then the second threshold was checked and so on. Only after all four entropy threshold parameters were met was traffic classified as distributed denial of service traffic. Jun et al. tested the entropy detection technique with a network simulator consisting of 19 nodes, 5 routers and 1 server and were successful at detecting distributed denial of service traffic during the simulation.

Aroua, Tunis and Zouari (2012) presented a new approach to detecting large-scale distributed denial of service attacks directed at national cyberspaces. Aroua et al. utilized the Saher architecture that was developed by the Tunisian Government to detect large-scale distributed denial of service attacks. The Saher architecture places sensors at all national Internet service providers and feeds information to a centralized server which analyzes traffic to determine if a large scale distributed denial of service attack is occurring. Aroua et al. determined the centralized server is a single point of failure and modified Saher to use a distributed solution wherein the probes also analyzed the traffic for distributed denial of service attacks. The probes communicated with each other and determined if distributed denial of service traffic was localized or occurring on a national level. Aroua et al. developed two responses for distributed denial of service attacks based on whether the distributed denial of service attack used reflector techniques or standard distributed denial of service attack techniques. A reflector distributed denial of service attack utilizes a botnet to send traffic to legitimate computers with a spoofed source IP address of the distributed denial of service target which causes the legitimate computers to flood the distributed denial of service target with traffic (Aroua et al., 2012). In contrast, standard distributed denial of service attacks send traffic straight from the botnet computers to the distributed denial of service target. For standard distributed denial of service attacks, Aroua et al. analyzed Internet ports and IP addresses to determine if a distributed denial of service attack was occurring and the probes then filtered offending IP addresses. For reflector attacks, Aroua et al. used the traffic rate observed at the border sensor to determine if an IP addresses was involved in a distributed denial of service attack and filtered IP addresses with traffic greater than a set threshold.

Ahirwal and Mahour (2012) developed an intrusion detection system to defend against distributed denial of service attacks in mobile adhoc networks. Ahirwal and Mahour's research is compelling because the testing used the NS-2 (2009) network simulator, and the intrusion detection system monitored outbound traffic, as well as inbound traffic. By monitoring traffic on one wireless node within the mobile adhoc network, Ahirwal and Mahour were able to detect and overcome a distributed denial of service attack. The NS-2 (2009) network simulator is a product of the Virtual Inter Networked Testbed, funded by the Defense Advanced Research Project Agency and developed by the University of Southern California, Xerox Palo Alto Research Center, Lawrence Berkeley National Laboratory and the University of California Berkeley.

Doyal, Zhan and Yu (2012) developed a technique to defend against distributed denial of service attacks that utilize IPSec tunnels to create an overlay network of authenticated clients. Doyal et al. called the technique Triple DoS and Triple Dos is only activated once a distributed denial of service attack is identified. Doyal et al. disbursed recovery units throughout the network and when the network was under a denial of service attack, the network clients established authenticated IPSec tunnel connections with a recovery unit. The recovery units also established IPSec tunnels to the edge of the network and traffic from the clients was routed through the recovery units to the edge of network, enabling the clients to bypass the denial of service attack and maintain Internet access (Doyal et al., 212).

Geva et al. (2013) reviewed bandwidth-distributed denial of service attack techniques, as well as the available defenses, and concluded new defense techniques are necessary to defend against distributed denial of service attacks. Bandwidth-distributed denial of service attacks are attacks executed by botnets, where the botnet sends a massive number of packets to the target to overwhelm the available bandwidth at the victim location (Geva et al., 2013). Geva et al. researched flooding attacks, reflection attacks, and amplification attacks. Through the research, the researchers determined a small botnet consisting of only 100 computers could execute a disturbed denial service attack that achieves 1Gb/s of traffic through a DNS amplification attack (Geva et al., 2013). A DNS amplification attack is a version of a reflection attack where botnets send DNS requests to open DNS servers with spoofed IP addresses, causing the DNS server to send responses to the victim, spoofed IP address (Deshpande, Katsaros, Basagiannis, & Smolka, 2011). Since many botnets have been discovered that contain millions of computers, the possible size of attacks is alarming (Geva et al., 2013).

Geva et al. (2013) reviewed the available defensive techniques to counter bandwidth-distributed denial of service attacks and determined new advanced techniques are required to counter the threat. Geva et al. researched rate limiting, filtering, access control lists, and other techniques to defend against distributed denial of service attacks, but they did not consider egress filtering at the source of the attack. Geva et al. noted that the best defenses against distributed denial of service attacks are implemented as close to the source of the attack as possible. Geva et al. stated distributed denial of service attack victims must be able to differentiate between the attack traffic and legitimate traffic to effectively mitigate an ongoing attack and defend against future attacks. Geva et al. recommended a response mechanism that filters attack traffic as close to the source as possible. Geva et al. stated victim locations are not able to effectively filter traffic during an attack because the network link is congested with data and regularly dropping network packets. Therefore, the traffic filter needs to be close to the source before the attack traffic is combined and causes congestion (Geva et al., 2013). Furthermore, Geva et al. recommended defense mechanisms be located close to the attacking sources. By locating the defense mechanism away from the victim and closer to the source of the attack, Geva et al. believed attack traffic will be identified and dropped by defense mechanisms, such as intrusion detection systems and routers, enabling only legitimate traffic to continue to the victim site.

Tao and Yu (2013) developed a distributed denial of service attack detection technique based on flow entropy at the local router and the Sibson distance of packets. Given two network flows with distributions of p(x) and q(x) "rather than take the average of both directions, the Sibson distance averages the KL distance from p(x) and q(x) to their average over each x" (Yu, James, Tian & Dou, 2012, p. 154). The KL distance is the relative entropy of two flows (Yu et al., 2012). Tao and Yu (2013) used the Sibson distance to overcome the problem of asymmetry when measuring network flows. Tao and Yu's technique is broken into two processes; the first determines when a small number of flows consume the majority of resources on the local router through an entropy algorithm. The second process is based on the Sibson distance the packets traveled and Tao and Yu added this process to distinguish between distributed denial of service attacks and flash crowds of legitimate network traffic. In their research, Tao and Yu pointed out flooding packet attacks are the most common and most powerful distributed denial of service attacks. Flooding packet attacks include SYN flood attacks and Tao and Yu's research supported the need for additional distributed denial of service attack countermeasures as presented in this study.

Yang et al. (2013) studied low-rate distributed denial of service attacks and determined low-rate distributed denial of service attacks are very difficult to detect. Yang et al. conducted experiments with low-rate attacks and were unable to detect the distributed denial of service attacks using current detection techniques, including signature-based techniques and threshold-based techniques. Although compromised computers in low-rate attacks send relatively small amounts of packets during attacks when compared to normal distributed denial of service attacks, the low-rate attacks are still able to produce up to one Gigabytes/sec in attack traffic (Yang et al., 2013). The information presented by Yang et al. showed that low-rate packets are requesting similar services and repeat attacks may use the same packet requests.

Ben-Porat et al. (2013) studied the difference between traditional distributed denial of service attacks and new sophisticated distributed denial of service attacks. Ben-Porat et al. stated that basic distributed denial of service attacks, such as high bandwidth attacks, simply send as much Internet traffic as possible to the target to overwhelm its available network resources. In contrast to basic distributed denial of service attacks, sophisticated distributed denial of service attacks attempt to overwhelm the target's computer resources by targeting weak points within computer system designs (Ben-Porat et al., 2013). Ben-Porat et al. highlighted the simple but effective SYN flood attack as a sophisticated distributed denial of service attack. Rather than target the bandwidth of the victim, the SYN flood attack targets the TCP stack and the handshake process (Ben-Porat et al., 2013). Ben-Porat et al. noted sophisticated distributed denial of service attacks allow attackers to use a smaller botnet and consume less bandwidth, which may allow those attacks to go unnoticed by traditional detection techniques.

Current Botnet Research

With the increase in peer-to-peer and decentralized botnets a majority of current research has focused on detecting peer-to-peer and decentralized botnets, in particular, the communications between bots within the botnet. Francois, Wang, Bronzi, State and Engel (2011) developed BotCloud to overcome the limitations of forensic analysis when examining large datasets of NetFlow data to detect peer-to-peer botnet communications. Francois et al. used Hadoop (Hadoop, 2013), an open source form of distributed computing based on Google's MapReduce (Dean & Ghemawat, 2004) to efficiently analyze NetFlow data. Similar to BotGrep (Nagaraja et al., 2010), Francois et al. developed BotCloud to identify peer-to-peer connections between hosts and identify botnet hosts utilizing an algorithm and graph analysis. BotCloud also showed improved detection rates when prior information about botnets is developed with a honeypot (Francois et al., 2011). Furthermore, BotCloud's use of Hadoop (2013) increased the efficiency and speed of botnet detection (Francois et al., 2011).

Zhang, Perdisci, Lee, Sarfraz and Luo (2011) developed a botnet detection technique to detect botnet peer-to-peer communications utilizing statistical fingerprints of peer-to-peer traffic. Peer-to-peer botnets have an advantage over IRC or HTTP protocol botnets because the former do not have a centralized command and control server and single point of failure (Zhang et al., 2011). The lack of a centralized command and control server make peer-to-peer botnets more resilient and more difficult to disable (Zhang et al., 2011). Zhang et al.'s peer-to-peer detection technique was focused on local area networks (LANS) and enterprise wide area networks (WANS); to detect peer-to-peer botnets. Zhang et al.'s technique first detects all peer-to-peer traffic and hosts and then develops signatures for different applications. Based on the signatures, Zhang et al. were able to differentiate legitimate peer-to-peer traffic from botnet peer-to-peer traffic. To develop the signatures of peer-to-peer traffic, Zhang et al. used the length of time a peer-to-peer program is operating because botnets run as long as possible and whenever a computer is turned on, while legitimate peer-to-peer programs are often started and stopped by the user. Based on the length of time a peer-to-peer program is active, Zhang et al. filtered out peer-to-peer hosts with short active times.

After filtering the peer-to-peer traffic based on length of active peer-to-peer traffic, Zhang et al. (2011) further differentiated the traffic based on IP addresses contacted by peer-to-peer hosts. Since peer-to-peer botnet hosts within the same LAN/WAN will often communicate with the same IP addresses and with other bots within the LAN/WAN, the researchers were able to filter out peer-to-peer hosts that did not communicate with any IP addresses that were not contacted by other peer-to-peer hosts(Zhang et al., 2011). The final filter Zhang et al. applied was based on the connection status of the traffic. If a peer-to-peer host had completed an outgoing three way handshake on a TCP connection or a UDP connection with a request and response packet, the traffic is kept and all other traffic is filtered out (Zhang et al., 2011). Zhang et al. based this filter on their findings that peer-to-peer nodes function as both a server and a client, and must accept connections from other hosts in the network and initiate connections with the same hosts. After this traffic filtering was complete, Zhang et al. attempted to identify peer-to-peer botnet hosts.

Zhang et al.'s final action to identify peer-to-peer botnet hosts involved differentiating between legitimate peer-to-peer traffic and botnet peer-to-peer traffic. To determine this, Zhang et al. analyzed the traffic for hosts that ran the same protocol and communicated with a high percentage of the same IP addresses. As stated earlier, bots of the same peer-to-peer botnet will communicate with each other and share IP destinations of other bots within the botnet. Furthermore, Zhang et al.'s research showed bots of the same botnet use the same peer-to-peer protocol. Based on these filters and detection techniques, Zhang et al. were able to detect 100% of the peer-to-peer bots within captured network traffic with only a 0.2% false positive rate.

Barthakur, Dahal and Ghose (2012) developed a procedure for detecting peer-to-peer botnet communications that is effective against encrypted communications, as well as HTTP traffic. Barthakur et al. used Support Vector Machines to analysis network traffic and classify botnet communications based on patterns and statistical differences between peer-to-peer botnet communications and normal web traffic. Barthakur et al. recognized botnet communications use many random ports and attempt to keep packet sizes to a minimum, which is the opposite of legitimate peer-to-peer to traffic. Based on these facts, Support Vector Machines were able to analyze patterns of peer-to-peer traffic and successfully identify botnet communications (Barhakur et al., 2012).

Han, Chen, Xu and Liang (2012) proposed a botnet detection and suppression system called Garlic. Han et al. believed Botmasters attempted to keep botnets as small possible to avoid detection and allow the Botmaster to easily change the botnet's command and control server. Han et al. stated the botnet suppression system, Garlic, was capable of automatically detecting and suppressing botnets. Han et al.'s Garlic suppression system relied on terminal nodes distributed throughout a network and the nodes collaborated with each other to detect patterns and alerts based on rules. Han et al. also observed that Garlic would regenerate rules based on feedback from the alerts and redistributed updated rules to the terminal nodes. During experimental testing, Han et al. were able to detect all 20 bots within 45 minutes; however, they only experimented with IRC botnets operating on TCP ports 6660-6669 (including IRC port 6667), as well as HTTP botnets operating on port 80. Han et al. did not test peer-to-peer botnet nor did they provide any research on peer-to-peer botnets within their study.

Yong, Tefera and Beshah (2012) developed a mathematical model to predict botnet growth and developed a framework based on the mathematical model to detect and mitigate botnets. Yong et al. predicted that 30% of all computers connected to the Internet are the maximum percentage of computers that could be infected by a botnet at any given time based on their mathematical model. Yong et al. believed the mathematical model can also be used to develop a framework for detection and mitigation of botnets. Yong et al.'s framework is similar to Gu et al.'s (2008) Botminer detection technique and proposes sensors located throughout a network and correlates alerts based on netflow data, as Botminer does with Botminer's C-Plane analyzer.

Zhang (2012) developed a new botnet detection technique to identify drive by download attacks and detecting botnets in the infection stage. Zhang recognized that many botnets use drive by downloads to infect new bots and by preventing the initial infection the size and scope of botnets could be greatly diminished. To identify drive by download techniques, Zhang collected HTTP traces from honeypots and whenever exploits were detected, the honeypots used a dynamic WebCrawler to record the URLs and IP addresses of the domains. Zhang then clustered groups of hostnames that share IP addresses. By clustering the hostnames based on shared IP addresses, Zhang was able to defeat the botnets that use fast flux network changes to command control server domain names and IP addresses. Fast flux networks use numerous IP addresses for one domain name and repeatedly update the DNS records for the domain name to different IP addresses to avoid detection (Caglayan, Toothaker, Drapaeau, & Burke, 2010).

Zhang (2012) also developed a system to increase the scalability of botnet detection systems. Zhang's system improved upon current detection systems by reducing the amount of packets requiring deep packet inspection; Zhang accomplished this by developing a three-step process that captures network flows, correlated the network flows and detected botnets through fine grain analysis. Rather than use deep packet inspection, Zhang's system used network flow information and packet header information, which allowed for deployments in larger networks and the ability to inspect traffic for botnet command and control traffic.

Zhang (2012) also developed a flow-capture process that monitors the edge of large networks and gathers netflow data on possible botnet traffic. The netflow data is then assembled and passed to the flow-correlation module. Zhang used a process developed in BotMiner called C-flow (Gu et al., 2008) to build the flow-correlation module. However, Zhang used a more efficient process for clustering netflows to allow for larger traffic volumes and employed correlation to identify hosts that had similar persistent communications. In Zhang's final process, a fine-grained detector utilizes previous detection techniques based on deep packet inspection. Zhang used both BotMiner and BotSniffer to inspect the traffic identified as possible botnet traffic by the flow-capture and flow-correlation modules and was able to achieve 100% detection rate when using cross correlation of flows and the B-sampling algorithm. For sampling rates above 0.05%, Zhang obtained false positive rates between 0.3% and 8%, as the sampling rate increased. However, when Zhang used both flow-correlation and a fine-grain detector, Zhang was able to detect 100% of botnets with no false positives for sampling rates above 0.05%.

Xiang, Binxing, Peng and Chaoge (2012) researched botnet communications and determined that previous research into the upload channel, i.e., communications from the botnet back to the botmaster, was lacking. Therefore, Xiang et al. proposed a botnet with a triple channel communications, or as they called it, a botnet triple-channel model. Xiang et al. reviewed current botnets, including IRC, HTTP, peer-to-peer, domain-flux, and URL flux botnet models, and determined that only IRC, HTTP, and domain-flux model botnets are capable of bi-directional communications with the botmasters. In other words, only bi-directional botnets have an upstream communications channel that is capable of uploading payloads, files, etc., directly to the Botmaster (Xiang et al., 2012). Xiang et al. maintained that future botnets would employ new bi-directional communications channels and that additional research is necessary to overcome advances in botnets with bi-directional communication capabilities.

Ilavarasan and Muthumanickam (2012) developed a two-stage detection technique aimed at detecting peer-to-peer botnets. Ilavarasan and Muthumanickam combined host level detection and network level analysis to overcome the limitations of each separately. The host level detection utilized registry analysis and file monitoring to detect changes related malware associated with botnets (Ilavarasan & Muthumanickam, 2012). Ilavarasan and Muthumanickam analyzed network traffic to identify peer-to-peer traffic and cluster similar traffic based on activity and contacted IP addresses. The final process in Ilavarasan's and Muthumanickam's detection technique was a correlation engine that combined the network analysis with the host level detection to alert for possible botnet infections.

Zeng (2012) developed a three-pronged approach to identify and mitigate the effects of botnets. Zeng proposed utilizing end host containment of infected bots, network edge detection of botnets, and measuring of network components at the infrastructure level for large botnet detection. Zeng also presented a proof of concept for future botnets utilizing mobile smart phones and SMS messages for command and control of a botnet. Zeng discussed the history of botnets and botnet detection techniques and highlighted the limitations of the current strategies to detect botnets. Most notably, the researcher discussed the rapidly changing communication methods for botnets, including peer-to-peer communications, and the limitations of current HTTP and IRC detection techniques (Zeng, 2012).

Zeng's (2012) research on end-host botnet detection incorporated previous techniques for containment of fast spreading network worms with new behavior analysis of all applications on the computer. The behavior analysis examined the actions of applications at the registry, file system and network stack, and was successful at identifying suspicious actions, while allowing legitimate applications (Zeng, 2012). Furthermore, the rate of false positives was greatly reduced when compared to existing detection techniques (Zeng, 2012)

Zeng (2012) also incorporated the edge network detection technique with the host-based detection to increase the effectiveness of botnet detection. The edge network detection utilizes NetFlow data captured from routers and does not access the packet payload, ensuring privacy for legitimate traffic (Zeng, 2012). Zeng identified 17 traits of botnets that he used to determine if network traffic was suspicious and related to botnets. The 17 traits identified by Zeng for botnet traffic include the following network features: mean, variance, skewness, and kurtosis for duration, total bytes, and number of packets. As well as the number of TCP flows, UDP flows, SMTP flows, unique IPs contacted, and number of suspicious ports (Zeng, 2012).

The final piece of Zeng's (2012) technique was botnet detection at the infrastructure level. Zeng chose to focus on large peer-to-peer botnets and evaluate the feasibility of detecting peer-to-peer botnets at the Internet infrastructure level. Zeng concluded that host-based techniques for botnet detection are not reliable and network edge detection is necessary to detect botnets. Furthermore, the behavior analysis and NetFlow analysis Zeng developed is independent of the type of botnet and command and control communication a botnet utilizes, thus it greatly increases the chances of botnet detection.

Li, Xie, Luo and Zhu (2013) developed a botnet detection technique based on botnet behaviors. Specifically, Li, Xie, et al. used six botnet behaviors to develop Snort (Cisco, 2014) alerts for botnet activity. The six behaviors that Li, Xie et al. (2013) determined were consistent with a botnet were: abnormal access to backup DNS servers, large number of domain name requests to a single domain, accessing fast flux networks, downloading malware, ingress and egress scanning, and null TCP connections. Every Snort alert was tracked in an alert matrix and correlated against the six known botnet behaviors to identify botnet activity (Li, Xie et al., 2013). Li, Xie et al. were successful at identifying 20 known botnets with detection rates between 74% and 94% with no false positives. Lie et al. also test the Snort (Cisco, 2014) rules against 8 unknown botnets and detected between 56% and 73% of unknown botnets with zero false positives. Lie, Xie et al. explain unknown botnets as botnets that the malicious behavior of the botnet is unknown, not the actual malware.

Alhomoud et al. (2013) proposed a self-healing system to detect botnets and counter the malware responsible for the botnet infections which would consist of five modules: the communication module, reporting module, detection module, healing module, and control module that would monitor the system and alert administrators to possible botnet infections, as well as take countermeasures. The self-healing countermeasures Alhomoud et al. proposed would include intercepting DNS queries, restoring registry changes, and as a last result removing the infected host from the network. Alhomound et al. only suggested the self-healing system in theory and did not construct nor test a self-healing system.

Cao and Qiu (2013) presented a formal definition and a framework for analyzing botnets at the 2013 IEEE Conference on Networking, Architecture and Storage. Cao and Qiu reviewed the existing definitions and developed a definition that incorporates three vital parts of a botnet, the botmaster, the bots, and the command and control technique, i.e., "The botnet is the distributed network with some unaware hosts under the remote control by the adversary" (p. 238). Cao and Qiu recommended six aspects of botnets to use when analyzing botnets: topology, communication protocol, control mechanism, command authentication mechanism, i.e., encryption, construction mechanism, i.e., how the malware is spread, and other mechanism. Cao and Qiu then used the proposed framework to analyze the SDbot, Waledac, and Andbot botnets.

Wang, Wang and Shi (2013) established a taxonomy to classify botnets according to the botnet's command and control structure. Wang et al.'s taxonomy is useful when researching botnets because the taxonomy provides a pattern for trends in botnets and assists researchers in finding weak points of botnets based on the botnet's command and control structure. Wang et al. believed peer-to-peer command and control structures provide the best resilience for botnets.

Rossow et al. (2013) studied peer-to-peer botnets for the peer-to-peer botnets resiliency and exposed vulnerabilities in eleven versions of peer-to-peer botnets that were still active on the Internet at the time of the research. Rossow et al. studied seven different versions of the *ZeroAccess* botnet, one version of the *Zeus* botnet, two versions of the *Sality* botnet and one version of the *Kelihos* botnet. They also reviewed five peer-to-peer botnets that had been abandoned or disabled, including *Nugache, Storm, Waledac,* two early versions of the *Kelihos* botnet, and the *Miner* botnet. Rossow et al.'s research determined the communication protocol, message propagation, direction of communications, purpose of each botnet, and the command and control architecture. The command and control architecture of the botnets were all peer-to-peer, but some of the botnets used other methods of command and control in earlier versions or still use other methods of command and control as a backup channel (Rossow et al., 2013). Rossow et al. found that peer-to-peer botnets are vulnerable to untrusted communications because they cannot use a secure authentication scheme between bots. Rossow et al. used the authentication vulnerability to propose mitigation and disabling techniques against each botnet and recommended future research on alternative peer-to-peer botnet mitigation techniques.

Rossow and Dietrich (2013) developed a system to detect encrypted botnet command and control communications. Rossow and Dietrich recognized that existing intrusion detection systems are not capable of detecting all encrypted command and control traffic based on payload signatures. The payload-based signatures used by intrusion detection systems are easily defeated by encrypted or obfuscated command and control traffic because botnets employ defense measures against payload signature recognition, such as dynamic encryption keys, data payloads encrypted with the XOR cipher, and varying the length of messages (Rossow & Dietrich, 2013). To counter the defenses employed by botnets, Rossow and Dietrich developed Provex, a Network Intrusion Detection system (NIDS), which detects encrypted botnet communications and was designed to learn from previously decrypted botnet communications and identify characteristic bytes within encrypted traffic. Then Provex "derives probabilistic vectorized signatures that can be used to verify if decrypted packets stem from a certain malware family's C&C" (Rossow & Dietrich, 2013, p. 6). Although Provex must decrypt network traffic and match signatures to the decrypted packets, Rossow and Dietrich were able to operate Provex at nearly 1Gbit/s of network traffic without packet loss and believed that Provex would handle network speeds of up to 10Gbit/s. In laboratory testing, Provex detected all true positive encrypted communications 100% of the time for six botnet variants and 78%, 81.5%, 87%, and 97% for four botnets, with only three false positive results (Rossow & Dietrich, 2013).

Garant and Lu (2013) developed a botnet detection technique to detect encrypted botnet communications within large networks. Garant and Le reviewed existing botnet detection techniques and determined existing techniques were ineffective against unknown botnets and botnets that employ encrypted communications. Grant and Lu developed the Weasel botnet that employs fully encrypted communications to test a new detection technique that is capable of detecting encrypted botnet communications and identified six features to identify the encrypted botnet communications: length in bytes, packet count, protocol, flow duration, flow direction, and TCP flags. To develop the signature of botnet communications utilizing the six features, Garant and Lu used a decision tree classification with the C4.5 and Weka's J48 algorithms; the researchers successfully detected over 90% of encrypted botnet communications with a false positive rate of 9.9% and false negative rate of 10.5%.

Conclusion

This literature review examined the existing research on botnet detection and distributed denial of service attacks in a chronological order. The review showed that botnets and botnet detection techniques are constantly evolving as Botmasters update and modify botnets to stay ahead of the latest botnet detection techniques (Alhomoud et al., 2013; Garant & Lu, 2013; Rossow et al., 2013; Zargar et al., 2013). Although IRC and HTTP botnets are still active, most new botnets use a decentralized infrastructure to avoid a single point of failure (Garant & Lu, 2013; Gu et al., 2009; Paxton et al., 2011; Rossow et al., 2013). Furthermore, a majority of botnets are now utilizing encrypted communications to avoid detection (Garant & Lu, 2013; Gu et al., 2009; Li, Xie et al., 2013; Paxton et al., 2011; Rossow & Dietrich, 2013; Rossow et al., 2013). Although many techniques exist to detect botnet communications within network traffic, those techniques rely on either packet decryption or real time analysis of all network traffic, both of which are resource-intensive (Gu et al., 2009; Paxton et al., 2011; Rossow & Dietrich, 2013). As botnets continue to employ advanced technologies, new pro-active detection techniques are required to counter the botnet threat (Dittrich, 2012; Gu et al., 2009; Paxton et al., 2011). It is expected that the pro-active botnet detection technique that characterizes distributed denial of service attacks and provides egress monitoring for Snort (Cisco, 2014) intrusion detection systems will detect botnets at the local network level, the source of the attack (Ben-Porat et al., 2013; Geva et al., 2013; Yang et al, 2013). Furthermore, new low bandwidth distributed denial of service attacks are able to evade many of the current detection techniques (Alomari, Manickam, Gupta, Karuppayah, & Alfaris, 2012; Ben-Porat et al., 2013; Yang et al, 2013). Characterizing low bandwidth distributed denial of service attacks, such as SYN flood attacks, will enable egress monitoring for attack packets and mitigation of low band-width distributed denial of service attacks (Alomari et al., 2012; Ben-Porat et al., 2013; Yang et al, 2013).

Summary

The literature review was necessary to ensure the research question had not yet been answered and justified the need for this study (Creswell, 2012). For this study, literature was reviewed from numerous sources including scholarly journals, conference papers, books, dissertations, and government documents. The literature was obtained from numerous online databases including, ProQuest, IEEE Computer Society Digital Library, Google Scholar, and the IEEE Xplore Digital Library. The keywords used in the search included *botnet, distributed denial of service, malware, denial of service, botnet detection, botnet identification, and proactive botnet.*

This literature review was conducted in a chronological order to show the evolution of botnets and botnet detection techniques and concluded with the latest botnet detection techniques. The review showed that original botnet detection techniques relied on passive honeypots and honeypots are not effective at detecting decentralized or encrypted botnets (Chen, Zhong, Chen, & Zhang, 2012; Feily et al., 2009; Leder et al., 2009; Rossow et al., 2013; Zeng, 2012; Zhang, 2012). Therefore, modern botnet detection techniques attempt to detect botnet command and control communications within network traffic (Brezo et al., 2011; Feily et al., 2009; Gu et al., 2007; Rossow & Dietrich, 2013; Rossow et al., 2013; Zeng, 2012; Zhang, 2012). The review showed a lack of research in the field of egress monitoring for botnet detection and also showed a need for tools to combat distributed denial of service attacks at the source of the attack.

Chapter 3 will cover the research method and design used for this study, as well as the experiment and data analysis.

CHAPTER 3: METHOD

The purpose of this quantitative quasi-experimental study was to investigate the extent to which the characteristics of distributed denial of service attacks, the Internet protocol, the Internet port, the TCP flags, and the flow rate of attack packets can be used to detect botnets as the botnet sends distributed denial of service attack packets. A sample distributed denial of service attack that was previously captured was used for the study. The captured distributed denial of service attack consisted of a 100MB packet capture of an actual distributed denial of service SYN flood attack launched by a variant of the *Black Energy* botnet. The packet capture consisted of 311,984 total packets, of which 47,548 were inbound SYN packets directed at the target web server as part of the distributed denial of service attack. Furthermore, a sample *Dark DDoSer* botnet was established in a controlled virtual environment for use in the study. The *Dark DDoSer* botnet was used to launch a SYN flood distributed denial of service attack and a packet capture of the attack was saved. The quasi-experimental study used one dependent variable, false positive detections of the distributed denial of service packets and four independent variables, the Internet protocol, the Internet port, the TCP flags, and the flow rate of attack packets. An initial concern was the feasibility of identifying independent variables that will reduce the number of false positive detections while still detecting actual distributed denial of service attack packets.

Data analysis for this experiment included the descriptive statistical measurements of mean, standard deviation, and range for the false positive alerts during the experiment. The number of false positives detections were reported for each independent variable, as well as for the combinations of independent variables as tested during the experiment. The results of the experiment were analyzed and interpreted with inferential statistical formulas including the Student's paired t-test and the repeated measures analysis of variance between groups, ANOVA, test. The paired t-test was used to compare the results of the experiment when utilizing one, two, three, or four independent variables. The repeated measures ANOVA test was used to interpret the results of all four groups together. The goal of the study was to manipulate the independent variables and affect the dependent variable until the experiment reports no false positives but still detects all distributed denial of service attack packets.

Research Method and Design Appropriateness

This study used a quantitative quasi-experimental research design to test the effectiveness of characterizing distributed denial of service attacks and detecting botnets through egress monitoring for the distributed denial of service characteristics. A quantitative research method was appropriate because the study examined how one variable influences another variable (Creswell, 2012). Creswell (2012) recommended quantitative research methods when the question under investigation attempts to explain how one variable influences another variable. Creswell (2012) also believed quasi-experimental designs are appropriate when studying a cause and effect relationship between variables. This study examined the relationship between four independent variables and one dependent variable and measured the cause and effect relationship between the variables (Creswell, 2012; Salkind, 2012). To test the cause and effect relationship between the variables, an experiment was performed on a personal computer. Creswell (2012) recommended the use of quantitative research methods for studies that require the use of instruments to collect numerical data and the use of statistics to analyze the results.

A quantitative research method was chosen for this study, rather than a qualitative or mixed method design. Creswell (2012) opined the use of qualitative research methods is preferred when research variables are unknown and the purpose of the study is to examine the central phenomenon of the research problem. According to Salkind (2012), qualitative research methods utilize personal interviews and surveys to collect data and statistical analysis is seldom used to interpret the data. Salkind also noted that qualitative research methods are best suited for social and behavioral science research.

Mixed method research designs use both quantitative and qualitative research methods in the same study (Creswell, 2012). According to Creswell, one reason to use a mixed method design is when the use of both quantitative and qualitative methods provide a better understanding of the research problem. Furthermore, mixed methods designs allow researchers to develop variables with qualitative methods and then use the variables in quantitative methods, and vice versa (Creswell & Plano Clark, 2011).

Quantitative research methods include survey designs, correlational designs and experimental designs (Creswell, 2012). Creswell stated that researchers use survey designs to collect data thru the use of questionnaires or interviews and interpret the results to describe trends. Survey designs do not manipulate variables to establish cause and effect between variables(Creswell, 2012). Correlational research designs are similar to survey designs, in that correlational designs do not establish cause and effect between variables (Creswell, 2012). However, correlational designs do measure the relationship between variables to determine if the variables influence other variables (Creswell, 2012).

According to Creswell (2012), an experimental research design determines if one variable causes an effect on another variable; the independent variable(s) are manipulated and the effect of the manipulation is measured on the dependent variable. If the dependent variable is affected by the procedure, then the independent variable is said to have caused the effect on the dependent variable (Creswell, 2012). Salkind (2012) stated true experiments require the random assignment of sample participants, which may not always be possible; therefore, quasi-experimental designs use intact groups or require the researcher to assign participants to groups.

A quantitative quasi-experimental design was chosen for this study to determine to what extent the characteristics of distributed denial of service attacks can be used to pro-actively detect botnets participating in distributed denial of service attacks. A quantitative research method was appropriate because the study examined how one variable influences another variable (Creswell, 2012). Furthermore, a quasi-experimental design was appropriate because the research problem called for a procedure to test a cause and effect relationship between four independent variables and one dependent variable (Creswell, 2012). Neither a qualitative nor mixed method research technique were appropriate for this study because neither method would answer the research question nor determine the independent variables effect on the dependent variable (Creswell, 2012; Salkind, 2012).

Research Question

Since this study used a quantitative quasi-experimental research design, the research question according to Creswell (2012) should relate the variables under investigation. Therefore, the research question asked. To what extent can the characteristics of a distributed denial of service attack (the Internet protocol, the Internet port, the TCP flags, and the flow rate of attack packets) be used to pro-actively detect botnets?

Hypothesis

For quantitative research, hypothesis should provide a prediction about the outcome of the research and the expected relationship between the variables (Creswell, 2009). For this study, the hypothesis states that characteristics of distributed denial of service attacks (the Internet protocol, the Internet port, the TCP flags, and the flow rate of attack packets) can be used to reduce false positive alerts for distributed denial of service attack packets while detecting botnets that participate in the distributed denial of service attack. Creswell (2009) explained that a null hypothesis makes a prediction that there is no relationship between the variables being studied. The null hypothesis for this study states that the characteristics of distributed denial of service attacks (the Internet protocol, the Internet port, the TCP flags, and the flow rate of attack packets) cannot be used to reduce false positive alerts for distributed denial of service attack packets while detecting botnets that participate in the distributed denial of service attack.

Variables

This study used a quasi-experimental design meant to test the possible cause and effect relationship between variables and according to Creswell (2012), experimental designs use independent and dependent variables to test cause and effect relationships. Salkind (2012) explained independent variables are treatments or conditions that are manipulated or changed by the researcher during an experiment. The four independent variables for this study were the Internet protocol, the Internet port, the TCP flags, and the flow rate of attack packets. Dependent variables on the other hand represent the observed result of an experiment, and the dependent variable may or may not be influenced by the independent variables (Salkind, 2012). The dependent variable for this study was the false positive alerts for the botnet's distributed denial of service attack packets as the packets egress the local area network.

Population

The population for this study consisted of fifteen packet captures of normal, non-malicious Internet traffic. The population was drawn from all internet traffic as a whole and are used to test for false positive alerts of the Snort intrusion detection system. The normal Internet packet captures were obtained from Garfinkel (2011) of the Naval Post Graduate School, and Ward (2009) of Cisco. Woods, Lee, Garfinkel, Dittrich, Russell, and Kearton (2011) created a set of realistic data captures for education and research use, titled M57-Patents, and Garfinkel (2011) made the packet captures available to the public on the website www.digitalcorpora.org. A screen capture of www.digitalcorpora.org with the public use disclaimer is provided in Appendix C. Seven of the available M57-Patents packet captures were used for this study. The data captures were selected at random and are shown in Table 2 (Garfinkel, 2011). Each data capture file consisted of 24 hours of network traffic (Garfinkel, 2011).

Table 2

M57-Patents Data Captures

Name	Packets	Size
net-2009-11-14-09_24.dmp	25813	6.5MB
net-2009-11-15-09_24.dmp	33773	11.2MB
net-2009-11-21-10_30.dmp	59813	51.2MB
net-2009-12-04-11_49.dmp	1686	1.7MB
net-2009-12-05-11_59.dmp	21066	4.5MB
net-2009-12-10-12_00.dmp	192932	150MB
net-2009-12-11-12_00.dmp	19974	9.6MB

Note. Adapted from Garfinkel's (2011) "Network packet dumps"

Ward (2009) titled his research "example.com" and provides the network captures

on his blog website, http://leonward.wordpress.com/2009/04/10/openpacketorg-

examplecom-pcap-files/. There are ten data captures; however, two data captures contain

malicious traffic, so only eight of the data captures were used for this study. An email

message from Ward approving the use of the data captures and the network diagram is

provided in appendix A. The eight data captures provided by Ward are listed in table 3.

Each example.com data capture is of different size and different duration.

Table 3

Example.com Data Captures

Name	Packets	Size
Example.com-1.pcap	4192	2.8MB
Example.com-2.pcap	14492	11.4MB
Example.com-3.pcap	2049	681KB
Example.com-4.pcap	9728	6.9MB
Example.com-5.pcap	1232	215KB
Example.com-6.pcap	4927	2.6MB
Example.com-7.pcap	1384	1MB
Example.com-8-overnight.pcap	129621	29MB

Note. Adapted from Ward's (2009) "example.com pcap files"

In addition to the fifteen non-malicious packet captures, two full packet captures of two distributed denial of service attacks were used in this study. The first distributed denial of service attack was a SYN flood distributed denial of service attack caused by the *Black Energy* botnet and a full packet capture of the attack packets was captured. The *Black Energy* distributed denial of service attack packet capture was 100 MB in size. A second SYN flood distributed denial of service attack was captured as part of this study. A sample *Dark DDoSer* botnet was constructed in a virtual environment and a SYN flood distributed denial of service attack was launched within the virtual environment. A full packet capture of the *Dark DDoSer* distributed denial of service attack was captured.

Sampling Frame

Salkind (2012) stated when a population is too large or diverse to study the entire population, then a researcher must create a subset, or sample of the population. For quantitative research designs Creswell (2012) recommended a sample size of 15 participants per group in an experiment, 30 participants for a correlational design and 350 participants for a survey while Salkind (2012) proposed at least 30 participants per group for a study. Both Creswell (2012) and Salkind (2012) have said that, in general, the larger the sample size the better the generalization of the study results will be and the less the sampling error. However, Salkind (2012) recommended only using the largest sample that is accurate and suitable for the study; over-sampling is simply a waste of time and resources. For this study, the sample size was based on Creswell's (2012) and Salkind's (2012) recommendations, and fifteen non-malicious Internet traffic packet captures and two distributed denial of service packet captures were used for the experiment. The number of packet captures, 17, meet Creswell's (2012) recommendation for sample size in an experiment, but Salkind (2012) recommended at least 30 participants per group. In this study, each packet capture consisted of at least 1000 individual packets, which can be considered participants for each group because the instrument, Snort (Cisco, 2014) actually tested every individual packet during the experiment. Therefore, this study meet the recommended sample size of both Creswell (2012) and Salkind (2012). The distributed denial of service attack samples consisted of 1000 individual network packets, and one sample was be developed from both the *Dark DDoSer* and *Black Energy* distributed denial of service attacks. The non-malicious Internet packet captures consisted of the full data captures as detailed in Table 2 and Table 3.

This study did not use any human participants and data collection did not involve any human subject participation such as interviews, surveys, or observation. Therefore, there were no confidentiality concerns for participants and it was not necessary to obtain informed consent of any individuals. There are no issues related to the geographic location of this study.

Data Collection

According to Creswell (2012), quantitative studies use instruments to measure variables and record the variables' response to change. Creswell also stated that quantitative instruments collect data in numerical format to enable the data to be analyzed with statistical tests. This study collected data during the experiment based on the Snort (Cisco, 2014) intrusion detection alerts as network packets were processed by the intrusion detection system. Data was collected in the form of correct detections, missed detections, and false positive detections for each run of the experiment based on the independent variables.

The experiment consisted of four separate procedures with each procedure utilizing a different number of independent variables, one through four respectively. Each procedure for the experiment used fifteen packet captures of non-malicious Internet traffic and two packet captures of the distributed denial of service attacks. The experiment used the software program Tcpreplay (Appneta, 2014) to replay the packet captures on the network. Erbarcher and Shevenell (2012) used tcpreplay to replay network captures and test intrusion detection systems including Snort. The number of false positive alerts was recorded during the non-malicious Internet traffic and the number of correct alerts was recorded during the distributed denial of service traffic.

The results of the experiment were analyzed and interpreted with statistical formulas including the Student's paired t-test and the repeated measures analysis of variance between groups, ANOVA, test. The paired t-test was used to compare the results of the experiment when utilizing one, two, three, or four independent variables. The repeated measures ANOVA test was used to interpret the results of all four groups together. Based on the results of the statistical procedures, the null hypothesis was either accepted or rejected. A procedural diagram for the data collection is shown in Figure 3.

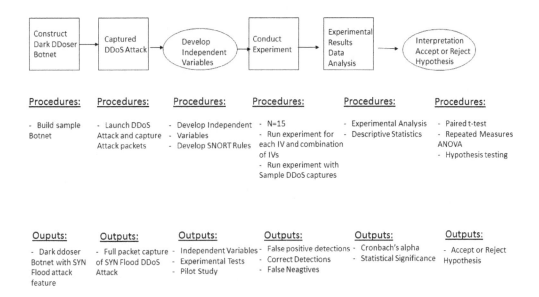

Figure 3. Procedural diagram of experiment, data collection and analysis

Instrumentation

This study examined botnet detection through distributed denial of service attacks carried out by botnets. The experiment monitored network traffic with the intrusion detection system, Snort (Cisco, 2014) and reported detections based on the independent variables. Creswell (2012) provided several criteria for selecting a good instrument, e.g., using the most recent version of an instrument and choosing an instrument that has been used by other researches in peer reviewed studies. Creswell also said to ensure the instrument will record the data required for the study and confirm the data is in the necessary format for the study.

The literature review provided a solid foundation for the use of Snort (Cisco, 2014) as an instrument for this study and confirms Snort's reliability. Gu et al. (2007), Gu, Perdisci et al. (2008), Gu, Zhang et al. (2008), and Li, Xie et al. (2013) all used Snort (Cisco, 2014) as an instrument for research on botnet detection. Kumar, Chandak and Dewanjee (2014) rated Snort as the best intrusion detection system in the *International Journal of Computer Applications.* Furthermore, an online search of the IEEE Computer Society digital library of peer reviewed journals and conference proceedings returned 1,078 unique articles that mention Snort (Cisco, 2014).

A pilot study is useful to test the instrumentation and determine if the instrument is valid and reliable (Leedy & Ormrod, 2012). Therefore, this study used a pilot study consisting of the software program Tcpreplay (Appneta, 2014) to validate the instrumentation and ensure Snort (Cisco, 2014) was reliable and installed correctly. The pilot study consisted of replaying 100 SYN packets from the Black Energy distributed denial of service attack and ensuring the packets were detected by Snort (Cisco, 2014) and replaying 100 UDP packets to ensure there were no false positive alerts.

Validity and Reliability

Quantitative experimental research designs use instruments to collect data in a numerical format and the instruments must report reliable and valid scores (Creswell, 2012). Salkind (2012) stated that validity is the confidence that an instrument accurately measures a test as intended, while Creswell (2012) observed that threats to validity must be addressed in experimental research to ensure the inferences drawn from the experiment are true. The inferences related to the design and execution of the experiment, and the relationships between the research variables are threats to the internal validity of a study (Creswell, 2012). Creswell (2012) observed that threats to internal validity are the most severe threats to the validity of a study because the internal validity effects the cause and effect relationships of the variables in experimental designs. However, the independent variables for this study, the Internet protocol, the Internet port, the TCP flags, and the flow rate of attack packets were drawn from actual distributed denial of service attack packets, and the same distributed denial of service attack packets were used in the experiment to test for correct detections. The independent variables were also used to test for false positive alerts against normal non-malicious Internet traffic and there is no way for the false positive alerts to influence the Snort (Cisco, 2014) rules. Consequently, a valid inference can be drawn between the variables, if the independent variables are shown to affect the dependent variable.

While internal validity relates to the instrumentation, variables, and the sample used for an experiment, external validity relates to the generalization of the study results and inferences drawn from the sample population to a larger population (Creswell, 2012). Creswell (2012) provided three threats to external validity and all three deal with treatment of the sample population, and how the sample population may differ from a larger population, making it difficult to generalize the results. The sample population for this study was packet captures of Internet traffic and there will be no treatment to the sample, so the external validity threats caused by any treatment were not of concern. The sample population's difference from a larger population was of possible concern; however, the threat caused by the sample size is covered by the limitations of the study as previously mentioned in Chapter 1. The results of this study are only applicable to SYN flood distributed denial of service attacks.

Salkind (2012) explained the relationship between reliability and validity, i.e., that reliability is a condition of validity. As such, tests can be reliable without being valid; however, tests cannot be valid without being reliable. Salkind said that tests are reliable when the outcome of the same test administered more than once produces the same result. In this study, the reliability and validity of Snort (Cisco, 2014) software is evidenced by the past use of Snort in many peer reviewed studies and dissertations with reliable and valid results (Gu et al., 2007; Gu, Zhang, et al., 2008; Gu, Perdisci, et al., 2008; Li, Xie et al., 2013).

Data Analysis

Data analysis in this study followed the five steps as outlined by Creswell (2012). Creswell noted the first step in data analysis is preparing the data, and includes scoring the data, choosing a statistical software program, and checking the database for errors. A descriptive analysis of the data was completed next and Creswell recommended measuring the central tendency and reporting variability. For this study, the descriptive analysis included the mean, mode, and median, as well as the variance, standard deviation and range for the experiment results. Salkind (2012) also recommended calculating the deviation from the mean and the squared deviation, but both of these calculations are part of the formula for the standard deviation, so only the standard deviation will be reported.

The next step, according to Creswell (2012), is to conduct inferential analysis, which can be used to test the hypothesis. For quantitative experiments, Creswell (2012) recommended the t-test and analysis of variance test. Since this study used repeated measures on groups of data, the paired t-test, also called the t-test for dependent means, and the repeated measures ANOVA test were used (Salkind, 2012). The paired t-test was used to test the hypothesis between experimental tests for the different number of independent variables (Creswell, 2012). Therefore, the paired t-test compared the results of test 1, which used a single independent variable, and test 2, which used two independent variables. Then the paired *t*-test compared test 2 with test 3, which used

three independent variables, and finally the paired *t*-test compared test 3 with test 4,

which used four independent variables. The repeated measures ANOVA test compared

the results of all tests with regards to the measurement of the dependent variable. The

level of significance for the paired *t*-test and the repeated measures ANOVA test were set

at alpha = 0.1 for this study. Thus, to reject the null hypothesis, that the probability of the

results are by chance, the p value of the respective paired *t*-tests, must be less than 0.1, *p*

< .1 (Creswell, 2012; Salkind, 2012). The repeated measures ANOVA test, often referred

to as the *f* test, uses the degrees of freedom between the groups of values and the degrees

of freedom for error to calculate the critical value of *f* (Hayter, 2012). The results of the

repeated measures ANOVA test were compared to the critical *f* value and if the *f* results

was greater than the *f* critical value, then the null hypothesis was rejected (Hayter, 2012).

Creswell (2012) also recommended reporting the results of the data analysis with

tables, graphs, and figures, and providing a discussion of the data analysis findings. The

fifth and final step in the data analysis, as recommended by Creswell, is to compare the

results with past studies and make suggestions for future research. This final step was

completed and is reported in Chapter 5 of the study.

Previous botnet detection techniques have reported varied success rates for botnet

detection and rates of false positive identification. Gu et al. (2007) reported a true

detection rate of 95.1% and a false negative rate of 4.9% during experimental honeynet

testing with only malicious traffic. During testing with captured network traffic and

injected malicious traffic, Gu et al. received a false positive rate of less than 0.1%, but Gu

et al. does not report a true detection rate.

Karasaridis et al. (2007) tested a passive botnet detection technique on selected sections of an ISP backbone network and reported a false positive rate of 2%. Karasaridis et al. did not a report a true detection rate nor false negative rate because the actual number of malicious packets was unknown. Gu, Perdisci, et al. (2008) tested Botminer with eight different botnets and reported a true detection rate of 100% for 6 of 8 botnets, and 75% and 99.6% for the other two botnets. The false positive rate for non-malicious traffic was less than 1% for 10 different days of testing. Wang and Yu (2009) were able to detect all botnet command and control communications in experimental testing with four botnet packet captures and obtained a false positive detection rate of 0.56% when testing with seven non-malicious packet captures.

Zeng et al. (2010) used both host level detection and network detection for a combined botnet detection technique. Zeng et al. used six botnet traces and one five day packet capture of non-malicious traffic for experimental testing. Zeng et al. obtained a false positive detection rate of 0.16% with only a single false negative missed detection during the experiment.

Francois et al. (2011) obtained an initial detection rate of over 99% and a false positive rate of 3% during initial testing. However, when Francois et al. used botnet data from a honeypot the detection rate stayed at 99%, but the false positive rate decreased to under 0.1%. Zhang et al. (2011) were able to detect 100% of 16 peer-to-peer botnets while only obtaining a false positive rate of 0.2%. Barthakur et al. (2012) obtained similar results for peer-to-peer botnet detection. Barthakur et al. detected 99.01% of botnet traffic and obtained false positive results of 0.11% for botnet traffic testing and 0.003% for non-malicious traffic testing.

Although the results of this study were analyzed with the paired t-test and the ANOVA test, the experimental testing results were also compared to past botnet detection techniques as reported in the previous paragraphs. The average detection rates for the eight studies listed above are 95.96% true positive, 0.79% false positive, and 2.5% false negative (Barthakur et al., 2012; Francois et al., 2011; Gu et al., 2007; Gu, Perdisci, et al., 2008; Karasaridis et al., 2007; Wang and Yu, 2009; Zeng et al., 2010; Zhang et al., 2011). The false negative rate was only reported in two studies so the accuracy of the 2.5% false negative rate is limited. Based on these statistics, the aim of this study was to have similar results of at least a 95% true positive detection rate and a false positive rate of less than 1%.

Summary

The purpose of this study was to examine to what extent the characteristics of a distributed denial of service attack can be used to detect botnets by identifying outgoing distributed denial of service attack packets at the point of origin. A quantitative quasi-experimental research design was chosen to test the cause and effect relationship between the independent and dependent variables (Creswell, 2012). The independent variables for this study consisted of the Internet protocol, the Internet port, the TCP flags, and the flow rate of attack packets. The dependent variable was the false positive alerts for the botnet's distributed denial of service attack packets as the packets egressed the local area network. The research population consisted of two packet captures from SYN flood distributed denial of service attacks and fifteen packets captures of non-malicious Internet traffic. The fifteen packets captures of non-malicious Internet traffic and two samples from the two packet captures of the distributed denial of service attack were the research samples.

The research samples were tested during an experiment with the intrusion detection software, Snort (Cisco, 2014) and the results were analyzed with descriptive and inferential statistics (Creswell, 2012, Salkind, 2012). Based on the inferential statistical results of the experiment, the hypothesis was accepted or rejected (Creswell, 2012).

CHAPTER 4: RESULTS

Overview

The purpose of this quantitative quasi-experimental study was to examine to what extent the characteristics of a distributed denial of service attack could be used to detect botnets that participate in distributed denial of service attacks through egress monitoring with the intrusion detection system, Snort (Cisco, 2014). Two distributed denial of service attack packet captures were characterized to develop the independent variables for this study. The study involved four independent variables (a) network protocol, (b) network port, (c) packet flags, and (d) rate of attack packets, as well as one dependent variable, false positive alerts for distributed denial of service attack packets.

A quasi-experiment was conducted with Snort (Cisco, 2014) to test the cause and effect relationship between the independent variables and the dependent variable. A total of eight different combinations of independent variables were tested with fifteen packet captures of non-malicious Internet traffic and two packet captures of distributed denial of service attacks. Through statistical analysis of the experimental results, this study tested one set of hypothesis. The research hypothesis states that characteristics of distributed denial of service attacks (the Internet protocol, the Internet port, the TCP flags, and the flow rate of attack packets) can be used to reduce false positive alerts for distributed denial of service attack packets while detecting botnets that participate in the distributed denial of service attack. Conversely, The null hypothesis for this study states that the characteristics of distributed denial of service attacks (the Internet protocol, the Internet port, the TCP flags, and the flow rate of attack packets) cannot be used to reduce false positive alerts for distributed denial of service attack packets while detecting botnets that participate in the distributed denial of service attack.

The statistical analysis of the collected data included both descriptive and inferential analysis. The descriptive statistical analysis included the mean, mode, and median, as well as the normality, variance, standard deviation and range for the experiment results. The study selected a level of significance and applied inferential statistics to the collected data. The inferential statistical analysis included the paired *t*-test and the repeated measures ANOVA test. The repeated measures ANOVA test was used to test the null hypothesis and the paired *t*-test was used to test the significance between the different combinations of independent variables. The non-parametric Friedman test and the Wilcoxon signed-rank test were also conducted. Microsoft Excel and SPSS software was used as the analysis software to compute the statistical analysis.

DDoS Analysis

To identify the independent variables for this study, two packet captures of SYN flood distributed denial of service attacks were analyzed. The first packet capture was from a SYN flood distributed denial of service attack caused by the *Black Energy* botnet. The second SYN flood distributed denial of service attack was captured as part of this study. A *Dark DDoSer* botnet was constructed in a virtual environment and a SYN flood distributed denial of service attack was launched within the virtual environment. During the *Dark DDoSer* distributed denial of service attack, a packet capture of the attack was created.

The two distributed denial of service attack packet captures were analyzed with the software program Wireshark (Wireshark Foundation, 2014). The analysis showed that both the *Black Energy* Botnet and the *Dark DDoser* Botnet used the TCP internet protocol to conduct distributed denial of service attacks. Furthermore, the analysis of the packet captures show that both botnets only used the SYN flag for attack packets and targeted port 80 as the destination port. The analysis of the distributed denial of service attack packet captures also determined the rate of attack packets sent by both botnets. The *Dark DDoser* Botnet sent a total of 108,496 SYN packets in 159 seconds during the attack. Since the *Dark DDoser* botnet was comprised of three computers, the average rate of attack packets was 227.45 packets per second by each computer. The *Black Energy* Botnet consisted of five computers and sent 222,953 SYN packets in 4136 seconds, giving an average rate of 10.78 SYN packets per second by each computer. Based on the mean rate of attack packets of the two distributed denial of service attacks, the rate of 10 packets per second was chosen as an independent variable. By using the lower of the two rates, it ensures future distributed denial of service attack carried out by either botnets will be detected. If the higher rate of 227 packets per second was used, then future Black Energy Botnet attacks may not be detected.

The four independent variables for this study were determined based on the analysis of the two distributed denial of service attacks. The independent variables chosen were (1) internet protocol TCP, (2) SYN flag, (3) port 80, and (4) flow rate of 10 packets per second. These four independent variables were then used to create Snort (Cisco, 2014) rules for use during the experiment. The Snort rules are shown in Table 4.

Table 4

Snort Rules based on the Independent Variables

Number of Independent Variables	Snort Rule
1	**TCP**, Internal IP, any -> External IP, any, none, none
2	**TCP**, Internal IP, any -> External IP, **80**, none, none
2	**TCP**, Internal IP, any -> External IP, any, **SYN**, none
2	**TCP**, Internal IP, any -> External IP, any, none, **10/sec**
3	**TCP**, Internal IP, any -> External IP, **80, SYN**, none
3	**TCP**, Internal IP, any -> External IP, **80**, none, **10/sec**
3	**TCP**, Internal IP, any -> External IP, any, **SYN, 10/sec**
4	**TCP**, Internal IP, any -> External IP, **80, SYN, 10/sec**

Note. The elements in bold are the independent variables being used for each test.

Pilot Study

A pilot study was conducted to ensure the validity and reliability of the instrument, Snort (Cisco, 2014), as well as the Snort rules. The pilot study consisted of eight executions of the data collection instrument Snort against one packet capture consisting of 100 packets taken from the *Black Energy* Botnet packet capture. Snort correctly identified the 100 attack packets during the three pilot tests that did not use the flow rate of attack packets as an independent variable. Snort also correctly identified the seven groups of 10 attack packets per second during the four pilot tests that used the flow rate of attack packets as an independent variable.

The pilot study also tested the reliability and validity of Snort for true negative and false positive detections. One packet capture consisting of 100 non-malicious UDP packets was used to test all eight Snort rules for non-malicious traffic. During all eight pilot tests for non-malicious traffic there were no Snort alerts. Therefore the results of non-malicious pilot testing show a 100% true negative response with zero false positives. Results from the pilot study supported the reliability and validity of Snort.

Findings

The experimental population for this study consisted of fifteen packet captures of normal, non-malicious Internet traffic, as well as two packet captures consisting of 1,000 packets taken from the distributed denial of service attacks. Each experimental population was tested with eight unique Snort (Cisco, 2014) rules consisting of one through four independent variables. The experimental procedure recorded the dependent variable, or number of false positive alerts for the non-malicious Internet traffic samples and true positive alerts for the distributed denial of service attack samples. The fifteen non-malicious packet captures were used to test the cause and effect of the independent variable on the dependent variable. The distributed denial of service attack samples were used to test the true detection rate and false negative rates of the Snort rules.

Descriptive Analysis

Creswell (2012) recommended displaying experimental results with descriptive statistics to describe trends in the data as related to independent variables. The study results are shown in Table 5 and Table 6, and are organized by independent variables to show the trends of each independent variable as related to the dependent variable, the number of false positive alerts. Table 5 shows the number of false positive alerts for each experiment and Table 6 lists the rate of false positive alerts, as a percentage of total packets sent. Based on the results shown in Table 6, the calculated rate of false positive alerts varies between a low of 0% and a high of 38.44% for the respective experimental procedures. The final experimental procedure that incorporated all four independent variables produced a total of 31 false positive alerts during the experiment, for an overall effective false positive alert rate of 0.0044%. Wireshark (Wireshark Foundation, 2014) was used to verify the number of false positive alerts detected by Snort (Cisco, 2014) was correct and the true negative percentage was 99.9956% with no false negative results.

Table 5

Experiment Results for Non-Malicious Internet Traffic

	Independent Variables							
	1	2-1	2-2	2-3	3-1	3-2	3-3	4
Packet Capture	False Positive Alerts							
example.com-1	1562	1548	56	125	56	125	0	0
example.com-2	4828	4758	134	419	130	417	2	1
example.com-3	357	331	37	20	37	19	0	0
example.com-4	3496	1622	179	288	97	125	2	2
example.com-5	87	0	0	0	0	0	0	0
example.com-6	1677	1600	110	143	107	140	1	1
example.com-7	532	514	15	35	15	35	0	0
example.com-8	14339	3531	281	375	241	295	4	4
net-2009-11-14-09	2710	2525	502	84	489	71	0	0
net-2009-11-15-09	5385	5081	685	247	663	221	0	0
net-2009-11-21-10	11982	11696	486	991	468	970	3	3
net-2009-12-04-11	461	20	3	41	3	1	0	0
net-2009-12-05-11	2060	1790	336	67	325	43	0	0
net-2009-12-10-12	62543	60870	2268	5205	2215	5077	20	20
net-2009-12-11-12	3768	3699	31	331	30	323	0	0

Table 6
Rate of False Positive Alerts

	Independent Variables							
	1	2-1	2-2	2-3	3-1	3-2	3-3	4
Packet Capture	False Positive Rate							
example1	37.26%	36.93%	1.34%	2.98%	1.34%	2.98%	0.00%	0.00%
example2	33.31%	32.83%	0.92%	2.89%	0.90%	2.88%	0.01%	0.01%
example3	17.42%	16.15%	1.81%	0.98%	1.81%	0.93%	0.00%	0.00%
example4	35.94%	16.67%	1.84%	2.96%	1.00%	1.28%	0.02%	0.02%
example5	7.06%	0.00%	0.00%	0.00%	0.00%	0.00%	0.00%	0.00%
example6	34.04%	32.47%	2.23%	2.90%	2.17%	2.84%	0.02%	0.02%
example7	38.44%	37.14%	1.08%	2.53%	1.08%	2.53%	0.00%	0.00%
example8	11.06%	2.72%	0.22%	0.29%	0.19%	0.23%	0.00%	0.00%
11-14-09	10.50%	9.78%	1.94%	0.33%	1.89%	0.28%	0.00%	0.00%
11-15-09	15.94%	15.04%	2.03%	0.73%	1.96%	0.65%	0.00%	0.00%
11-21-10	20.03%	19.55%	0.81%	1.66%	0.78%	1.62%	0.01%	0.01%
12-04-11	27.34%	1.19%	0.18%	2.43%	0.18%	0.06%	0.00%	0.00%
12-05-11	9.78%	8.50%	1.59%	0.32%	1.54%	0.20%	0.00%	0.00%
12-10-12	32.42%	31.55%	1.18%	2.70%	1.15%	2.63%	0.01%	0.01%
12-11-12	18.86%	18.52%	0.16%	1.66%	0.15%	1.62%	0.00%	0.00%
Average	23.29%	18.60%	1.16%	1.69%	1.08%	1.38%	0.0049%	0.0044%

A 100% true positive detection rate was achieved for both packet captures across all eight experimental procedures. Although the number of independent variables was increased from one to four, there was no reduction in correct detections. However, the corresponding false positive rates were greatly reduced. The results of the true positive detections are shown in Table 7.

Table 7

Experiment Results for DDoS Traffic

Number of Independent Variables	Snort Rule	Black Energy	Dark DDoSer
		True Positive Alerts	
1	**TCP**, Internal IP-any, External IP, any, none, none	1000	1000
2	**TCP**, Internal IP-any, External IP, **80**, none, none	1000	1000
2	**TCP**, Internal IP-any, External IP, any, **SYN**, none	1000	1000
2	**TCP**, Internal IP-any, External IP, any, none, **10/sec**	70	99
3	**TCP**, Internal IP-any, External IP, **80, SYN**, none	1000	1000
3	**TCP**, Internal IP-any, External IP, **80**, none, **10/sec**	70	99
3	**TCP**, Internal IP-any, External IP, any, **SYN, 10/sec**	70	99
4	**TCP**, Internal IP-any, External IP, **80, SYN, 10/sec**	70	99

Note. The elements in bold are the independent variables being used for each test.

Creswell (2012) also recommended using descriptive statistics to show general tendencies in the experimental results. Additional descriptive statistics measured in this study included the mean, median, range, standard deviation, and sample variance for the number of false positive alerts observed during each experimental procedure. The descriptive statistics and data ranges for the eight experimental procedures are summarized in Tables 8 and 9.

Furthermore, the experimental results were tested for normality with the Shapiro-Wilk test. The false positive results were not normally distributed as assessed by the Shapiro-Wilk's test ($p < 0.1$). Given the fact the repeated measures ANOVA test is fairly robust to deviations from normality, the results were all similarly skewed, and that non-normality does not substantially affect type I error rates the repeated measures ANOVA and paired t-test were still used as a statistic in this study. However, for an abundance of

caution the non-parametric equivalent statistic tests, the Friedman test and the Wilcoxon

signed-rank test were also completed.

Table 8
Data Ranges for Number of False Positive Alerts

Variable	Range	Minimum Range	Maximum Range
IV 1	62456.00	87.00	62543.00
IV 2-1	60870.00	0	60870.00
IV 2-2	2268.00	0	2268.00
IV 2-3	5205.00	0	5205.00
IV 3-1	2215.00	0	2215.00
IV 3-2	5077.00	0	5077.00
IV 3-3	20.00	0	20.00
IV 4	20.00	0	20.00

Table 9
Descriptive Statistics for Number of False Positive Alerts

Variable	M	Mdn	SD	S
IV 1	7,719.13	2,710.00	15,728.10	247,373,206.27
IV 2-1	6,639.00	1,790.00	15,289.95	233,782,518.43
IV 2-2	341.53	134.00	573.91	329,373.41
IV 2-3	558.07	143.00	1,309.94	1,715,939.64
IV 3-1	325.07	107.00	562.27	316,144.07
IV 3-2	524.13	125.00	1,283.68	1,647,821.70
IV 3-3	2.13	0.00	5.11	26.12
IV 4	2.07	0.00	5.12	26.21

Inferential Analysis

For quantitative experiments, Creswell (2012) recommended the t-test and

analysis of variance test for inferential analysis and testing the hypothesis. Since this study investigated the differences in mean scores under eight different conditions the repeated measures ANOVA test and the paired t-test were used (Salkind, 2012). This study applied a repeated measures analysis of variance (ANOVA) statistic to the results of the experimental procedure and used an alpha value of 0.1. The repeated measures ANOVA test compared the results of all eight repeated measurements with regards to the measurement of the dependent variable, the number of false positive alerts. The null hypothesis was rejected if the F value was greater than the critical F value. In addition to the repeated measures ANOVA test, a paired t-test was applied to the experimental results for pairs of independent variables to test the significance between the different sets of independent variables. During the paired t-tests, the statistic used an alpha value of 0.1. The non-parametric Friedman test and the Wilcoxon signed-rank test were also conducted to ensure the normality of the data was not an issue with the repeated measures ANOVA test and paired t-test.

Paired t-test. The level of statistical significance was measured between the sets of independent variables with a paired t-test. An alpha value of 0.1 was used for the paired t-tests, therefore a p value of less than 0.1 indicates the null hypothesis is false. For the experimental procedures consisting of two and three independent variables, the average value of the dependent variable response were used for the paired t-test.

The results of the paired t-tests are summarized in Tables 10 through 13. Examination of the experimental results reveal a significant difference between independent variable 1 and the average of independent variable 2, as well as between the average of independent variable 2 and independent variable 3, and independent variable 3 and independent variable 4. Overall the difference between independent variable 1 and 4, also show a statistically significance difference. Evaluation of the p value = 0.039,

supports the rejection of the null hypothesis.

Table 10
Paired t-test between IV 1 and IV 2

Groups	N	M	S	df	t	p
Independent Variable 1	15	7,719.1333	247,373,206			
				14	1.9874	0.0333
Independent Variable 2	15	2,512.8667	32,666,421.3			

Note. Significant at $p < 0.1$.

Table 11
Paired t-test between IV 2 and IV 3

Groups	N	M	S	df	t	p
Independent Variable 2	15	2,512.867	32,666,421.31			
				14	1.6904	0.0565
Independent Variable 3	15	283.778	371,178.42			

Note. Significant at $p < 0.1$.

Table 12
Paired t-test between IV 3 and IV 4

Groups	N	M	S	df	t	p
Independent Variable 3	15	283.778	371,178.42			
				14	1.8056	0.0462
Independent Variable 4	15	2.0667	26.209			

Note. Significant at $p < 0.1$.

Table 13

Paired t-test between IV 1 and IV 4

Groups	N	M	S	df	t	p
Independent Variable 1	15	7,719.133	247,373,206.3			
				14	1.9009	0.03905
Independent Variable 4	15	2.0667	26.209			

Note. Significant at $p < 0.1$.

Wilcoxon signed-rank test. Since the experimental results were not normally distributed the non-parametric Wilcoxon signed-rank test was also completed to ensure the violation of normality did not affect the paired t-test. The Wilcoxon signed-rank test does not have an assumption of normality. The Wilcoxon signed-rank test confirmed the results of the paired t-test and showed a greater leave of significance between the variables. The statistical result between independent variable 1 and the average of independent variable 2 was ($Z = -3.408, p = 0.001$). The statistical result between the average of independent variable 2 and independent variable 3 was ($Z = -3.296, p = 0.001$), and between the average of independent variable 3 and independent variable 4 was ($Z = -3.296, p = 0.001$). Overall the difference between independent variable 1 and independent variable 4 was ($Z = -3.408, p = 0.001$). Evaluation of the p value $= 0.001$, supports the rejection of the null hypothesis.

Repeated measures ANOVA. The results of the experiment were statistically significant relative to all four independent variables. A repeated measures ANOVA was used to test the null hypothesis. One hundred and twenty measurements were performed according to the experimental procedure; eight measurements for each of the fifteen sample populations. The dependent variable had a possible range of zero to n, where n is the total number of packets in each sample packet capture. The results of the experiment were organized by dependent variable and are recorded as shown in Table 5. The results

of the repeated measures ANOVA are provided in Table 14 and the *F* value was greater

than the *F* critical value, so the null hypothesis was rejected. Based on the *F* value, $F(7,$

$14) = 3.21$, $p = 0.004$, the treatment of the independent variables on the sample

populations had a significant effect on the dependent variable.

Table 14
Repeated Measures ANOVA

	N	Sum	M	S
IV 1	15	115,787	7,719.13	247,000,000
IV 2-1	15	99,585	6639	234,000,000
IV 2-2	15	5,123	341.53	329,373.4
IV 2-3	15	8,371	558.06	1715,940
IV 3-1	15	4,876	325.06	316,144.1
IV 3-2	15	7,862	524.13	1647,822
IV 3-3	15	32	2.13	26.12
IV 4	15	31	2.06	26.20

Source of Variation	SS	df	MS	F	P-value	F crit
IV1 – IV4	1,080,000,000	7	154,000,000	3.218068	0.004108	1.779028

Note: Significant at $F > F$ crit.

The repeated measures ANOVA test assumes sphericity, that the variances of the

difference between conditions are equal. Therefore, a Mauchly test was conducted on the

data and the test indicated that the assumption of sphericity had been violated, $X^2(27) =$

775.1, $p < .001$ ($p = 7.74e\text{-}144$). However, sphericity is often violated with repeated

measures ANOVAs, so Greenhouse and Geisser (1959) develop a procedure to correct

for sphericity violations that lowers the degrees of freedom of the F-distribution. Using

the Greenhouse-Geisser correction, the repeated ANOVA test showed an increased *p*

value of 0.093, which is less than alpha of 0.10 and the F value remained greater than the

F critical value, so the null hypothesis was rejected. Table 15 shows the results of the

Repeated Measures ANOVA Test with the Greenhouse-Geiser Correction.

Table 15

Repeated Measures ANOVA Test with Greenhouse-Geisser Correction

Source of Variation	SS	df	MS	F	P-value	F crit
IV1 – IV4	1,080,000,000	7	154,000,000	3.218068	0.093	1.779028

Note: Significant at *F > F* crit.

Friedman test. Since the experimental results were not normally distributed the

non-parametric Friedman test was also completed to ensure the violation of normality did

not affect the repeated measures ANOVA. The Friedman test does not have an

assumption of normality. The Friedman test confirmed the results of the repeated

measures ANOVA and showed there was a statistically significant difference in the

number of false positive alerts between the independent variables, $X^2(7) = 91.8$, $p < .001$

($p = 5.27E\text{-}17$) and the null hypothesis was rejected.

Summary

The purpose of this quantitative quasi-experimental study was to examine to what

extent the characteristics of a distributed denial of service attack could be used to detect

botnets that participate in distributed denial of service attacks through egress monitoring

with the intrusion detection system, Snort (Cisco, 2014). Results of the experimental

testing were analyzed with both descriptive and inferential statistics. A significant

reduction in the dependent variable, the number of false positive Snort alerts was

observed as the independent variables were increased from one to four. The final rate of

false positive alerts was 0.0044%. While at the same time, the true detection rate of distributed denial of service attack packets that were egressing from the network was 100%.

A repeated measures ANOVA test was conducted to examine the cause and effect relationship between the four independent variables and the dependent variable. A significant statistical difference was measured with the repeated measures ANOVA test and the null hypothesis was rejected. Thus, the research hypothesis was accepted and it states that characteristics of distributed denial of service attacks (the Internet protocol, the Internet port, the TCP flags, and the flow rate of attack packets) can be used to reduce false positive alerts for distributed denial of service attack packets while detecting botnets that participate in the distributed denial of service attack.

Inferential analysis was also conducted with a paired *t*-test to measure the statistical significance between the different independent variables. The null hypothesis was rejected for all comparisons of independent variables. Also, the overall comparison between independent variables 1 and 4 was statistically significant and rejected the null hypothesis.

The non-parametric Friedman test and the Wilcoxon signed-rank test were also conducted to ensure the normality of the data was not an issue with the repeated measures ANOVA test and paired t-test. The Friedman test confirmed the results of the repeated measures ANOVA and showed there was a statistically significant difference in the number of false positive alerts between the independent variables, $X^2(7) = 91.8, p < .001$ ($p = 5.27E\text{-}17$) and the null hypothesis was rejected. The Wilcoxon signed-rank test also confirmed the results of the paired t-tests and null hypothesis was rejected. Interpretations and recommendations are further discussed in Chapter 5.

CHAPTER 5: CONCLUSIONS AND RECOMMENDATIONS

According to Zargar, Joshi and Tipper (2013) distributed denial of service attacks conducted by botnets are one of the largest concerns for Information Assurance Professionals and a new defense mechanism is needed to protect networks against distributed denial of service flooding attacks. The best way to defend against distributed denial of service attacks is to stop the attack closer to the origin of the attack (Zargar et al., 2013). If a new botnet detection technique can be developed that is able to detect distributed denial of service attacks at the point of origin, the technique will improve botnet detection and enhance mitigation of attacks (Zargar et al., 2013).

The purpose of this quantitative quasi-experimental study was to examine to what extent the characteristics of a distributed denial of service attack could be used to detect botnets that participate in distributed denial of service attacks through egress monitoring with the intrusion detection system, Snort (Cisco, 2014). Two distributed denial of service attacks were characterized to develop the independent variables for this study and one dependent variable was measured. A repeated measures analysis of variance (ANOVA) statistic was used to measure the statistical significance of the experiment as a whole and a paired t-test was used to measure the statistical significance of the treatment between the independent variables. The non-parametric Friedman test and the Wilcoxon signed-rank test were also conducted to ensure the normality of the data was not an issue with the repeated measures ANOVA test and paired t-test.

Limitations

This study was limited in size and scope. The research used a previously captured *Black Energy* distributed denial of service attack and a *Dark DDoSer* distributed denial of service attack that was created as part of the study. Both distributed denial of service attacks were SYN flood attacks, therefore the scope of this study is limited to SYN flood distributed denial of service attacks. Botnets that execute reflective distributed denial of service attacks and DNS amplification distributed denial of service attacks are beyond the scope of this study since both attacks involve the use of third party computers or DNS servers to send the actual attack packets to the victim computer (Kline, Beaumont-Gay, Mirkovic, & Reiher, 2009; Meenakshi, Raghavan, & Bhaskar, 2011).

Study Taxonomy

The literature reviewed for this study was drawn from numerous databases including: ProQuest, IEEE Computer Society Digital Library, Google Scholar, and the IEEE Xplore Digital Library. Numerous search phrases and keywords were used in the search and a complete list of search terms is available in Appendix D. The literature review was conducted in a chronological order to show the evolution of botnets and botnet detection techniques. The literature review showed botnets and distributed denial of service attacks are constantly evolving and there is ample opportunity to contribute to the field of botnet detection. A total of 197 peer reviewed articles, 22 studies (including dissertation and thesis papers), 29 books, and 110 germinal works were used to contribute to this study. Of these works, a total of 95 were referenced and cited in this study.

Findings and Interpretations

This study applied a repeated measures analysis of variance (ANOVA) statistic to assess the cause and effect relationship between the four independent variables and the dependent variable. Results of the repeated measures ANOVA are provided in Table 11 and reveal a significant statistical relationship between the variables. The F value was equal to 3.21, which is greater than the F critical of 2.10, and $p = 0.0041$, which is less than the established alpha value of 0.1, all of which show a strong statistical relationship between the variables with a confidence level of 90%. These results reject the null hypothesis and accept the research hypothesis, which states the characteristics of distributed denial of service attacks (the Internet protocol, the Internet port, the TCP flags, and the flow rate of attack packets) can be used to reduce false positive alerts for distributed denial of service attack packets while detecting botnets that participate in the distributed denial of service attack.

Inferential analysis was also conducted with a paired t-test to measure the statistical significance between the different independent variables. The null hypothesis was rejected for all comparisons of independent variables. The non-parametric Friedman test and the Wilcoxon signed-rank test were also conducted to ensure the normality of the data was not an issue with the repeated measures ANOVA test and paired t-test. Both the Friedman test and the Wilcoxon signed-rank test rejected the null hypothesis. While the inferential analysis is important to test the set of hypothesis used in this study, previous studies have reported the false positive rate and true positive rate in their findings.

Previous botnet detection techniques have reported varied success rates for botnet detection and rates of false positive identifications. The average detection rates for eight studies reviewed as part of this study were 95.96% true positive and 0.79% false positive (Barthakur et al., 2012; Francois et al., 2011; Gu et al., 2007; Gu, Perdisci, et al., 2008; Karasaridis et al., 2007; Wang and Yu, 2009; Zeng et al., 2010; Zhang et al., 2011). The false positive rate for this study was 0.0044%, and the true positive rate was 100%. These rates show this detection technique is above average when compared to previous detection techniques. Table 16 shows the true detection rates and false positive detection rates for eight studies reviewed as part of this study.

Table 16
Previous Detection Rates

Researchers	True Detection Rate	False Positive Rate
Gu et al. (2007)	95.1%	0.049%
Karasaridis et al. (2007)	Not reported	2%
Gu, Perdisci et al. (2008)	96.83%	0.0003%
Wang and Yu (2009)	100%	0.0056%
Zeng et al. (2010)	99.99%	0.16%
Francois et al. (2011)	99%	0.1%
Zhang et al. (2011)	100%	0.2%
Barthakur et al. (2012)	99.01%	0.11%
Average of Above	95.56%	0.79%
Hyslip (2014)	100%	0.0044%

Note. Gu, Perdisci et al. (2008) true detection rate is an average of 8 tests

Recommendations

The results of this study, combined with the literature review, exposed opportunities for Information Security Researchers to conduct research focused on botnet detection techniques aimed at egress monitoring. The potential exists to characterize many types of distributed denial of service attacks and establish intrusion detection system rules to detect attack packets as the packets egress the network. By detecting the attack packets at the point of origin, rather than at the destination of the attack, this technique has the potential to greatly reduce the effectiveness of distributed denial of service attacks, while detecting the computers participating in the attack, that are members of a botnet. Since the majority of corporations and government agencies already employ intrusion detection systems, the egress monitoring rules developed in this study can be easily implemented by a large number of Internet users.

The findings of this study may also be of value to civilian law enforcement agencies and intelligence agencies. The pro-active technique of covertly ordering a distributed denial of service attack against a server that is controlled by law enforcement or intelligence agencies will enable authorities to identify the infected computers that are members of the attacking botnet. Furthermore, the Botmaster's mode of communication and payment method may be identified, and the distributed denial of service attack can be attributed to the Botmaster.

Recommendations for Future Research

Using this study as a guide, additional research should be done to characterize additional types of distributed denial of service attacks carried out by botnets. Ben-Porat et al. (2013) discussed different types of sophisticated low bandwidth distributed denial of service attacks that attack computer system hardware and protocols rather than simply overwhelming the available bandwidth. These types of distributed denial of service attacks would be ideal for characterization because the attacks use specific requests or protocols. The characteristics of the attacks could then be used to develop new rules for egressing monitoring.

Since this study was conducted in a closed network environment with packet captures, future research should be done to test this technique on live networks. Depending on the size of the network, numerous intrusion detection sensors may be required. If a single sensor was placed at the gateway of a large network, the sensor may be overwhelmed. Furthermore, if network address translation is used inside a network, the sensor may see many users on one subnet as a single user and alert to their activity, rather than that of a single computer. Therefore, additional research is required on different size networks to test the technique.

Summary

This study showed that the characteristics of a distributed denial of service attack can be used to pro-actively detect botnets. Through a quasi-experiment using four independent variables developed from actual distributed denial of service attacks, the measured effect on the dependent variable was shown to have been caused by the experimental treatment. Therefore, the null hypothesis was rejected and the research hypothesis which states, the characteristics of distributed denial of service attacks (the Internet protocol, the Internet port, the TCP flags, and the flow rate of attack packets) can be used to reduce false positive alerts for distributed denial of service attack packets while detecting botnets that participate in the distributed denial of service attack, was accepted. Although limitations were present in the research, the results are significant for the manner in which the study used egress monitoring for botnet detection.

The findings of the study also showed that characterization of a distributed denial of service attack as a technique for botnet detection is more effective than previous botnet detection techniques reviewed for this study. Combined, the 100% true detection rate and 0.0044% false positive rate where equal to or better than all detection rates reviewed for this study. The hope is that this study serves as motivation for additional research into the characterization of distributed denial of service attacks and egress monitoring as a botnet detection technique.

REFERENCES

Ahirwal, R., & Mahour, L. (2012). Analysis of distributed denial of service attack effect and protection scheme in wireless mobile ad-hoc network. *International Journal on Computer Science & Engineering, 4*(6), 1164-1173. Retrieved from http://www.enggjournals.com/ijcse/doc/IJCSE12-04-06-162.pdf

Alhomoud, A., Awan, I., Disso, J., & Younas, M. (2013). A next-generation approach to combating botnets. *Computer, 46*(4), 62-66. Retrieved from http://doi.ieeecomputersociety.org/10.1109/MC.2013.67

Alomari, E., Manickam, S., Gupta, B., Karuppayah, S., & Alfaris, R. (2012). Botnet-based distributed denial of service (DDoS) attacks on web server: Classification and art. *International Journal of Computer Applications, 47*(7), 24-32. doi: 10.5120/7640-0724

Andriesse, D., Rossow, C., Stone-Gross, B., Plohmann, D., & Bos, H. (2013, October). Highly resilient peer-topeer botnets are here: An analysis of gameover zeus. *Proceedings of the 8th International Conference on Malicious and Unwanted Software: "The Americas" (MALWARE),* Pajardo, PR, 116-123. Retrieved from http://doi.ieeecomputersociety.org/10.1109/MALWARE.2013.6703693

Appneta (2014). Tcpreplay (Version 4.0) [Computer Software]. Boston, MA: Author.

Aroua, M., Tunis, T., & Zouari, B. (2012, July). A distributed and coordinated massive distributed denial of service attack detection and response approach. *Proceedings of the 2012 IEEE 36th International Conference on Computer Software and Applications Workshops*, Izmir, Turkey, 230-235. Retrieved from http://dx.doi.org/10.1109/COMPSACW.2012.50

Barthakur, P., Dahal, M., & Ghose, M. (2012, October). A framework for peer-to-peer botnet detection using SVM. *Proceedings of the 2012 International Conference on Cyber-Enabled Distributed Computing and Knowledge Discovery*, Sanya, China, 195-200. Retrieved from http://doi.ieeecomputersociety.org/10.1109/CyberC.2012.40

Ben-Porat, U., Bremler-Barr, A., & Levy, H. (2013). Vulnerability of network mechanisms to sophisticated ddos attacks. *IEEE Transactions on Computers, 62*(5), 1031-1043. Retrieved from http://doi.ieeecomputersociety.org/10.1109/TC.2012.49

Bijalwan, A., Thapaliyal, M., Pilli, E., & Joshi, R. (2013). Survey and research challenges of botnet forensics. *International Journal of Computer Applications, 75*(7), 43-50. doi: 10.5120/13127-0483

Brezo, F., Santos, I., Bringas, P., & Val, J. (2011, Aug). Challenges and limitations in current botnet detection. *Proceedings of the 22nd International Workshop on Database and Expert Systems Applications,* Toulouse, France, 95-101. Retrieved from http://dx.doi.org/10.1109/DEXA.2011.19

Caglayan, A., Toothaker, M., Drapaeau, D., & Burke, D. (2010, January). Behavioral patterns of fast flux service networks. *Proceedings of the 2010 43rd Hawaii International Conference on System Sciences (HICSS)*, Honolulu, HI, 1-9. doi: 10.1109/HICSS.2010.81

Cao, L, & Qiu, X. (2013, July). Defense against botnets: A formal definition and a general framework. *Proceedings of the 2013 IEEE Eighth International Conference on Networking, Architecture, and Storage*, Xi'an, Shaanxi, China,

237-241. Retrieved from

http://doi.ieeecomputersociety.org/10.1109/NAS.2013.37

Chen, J., Zhong, M., Chen, F., & Zhang, A. (2012, August). DDoS defense system with

turing test and neural network. *Proceedings of the 2012 IEEE International*

Conference on Granular Computing, Hangzhou, China, 38-43. Retrieved from

http://doi.ieeecomputersociety.org/10.1109/GrC.2012.6468680

Cisco. (2014). Snort (Version 2.9.6.2) [Computer Software]. Retrieved from

http://www.snort.org/downloads

Cooke, E., Jahanian, F., & McPherson, D. (2005, July). The zombie roundup:

Understanding, detecting, and disrupting botnets. *Proceedings of the Steps to*

Reducing Unwanted Traffic on the Internet Workshop 2005, Cambridge, MA.

Retrieved from

https://www.usenix.org/legacy/events/sruti05/tech/full_papers/cooke/cooke.pdf

Cottrell, R., & McKenzie, J. (2010). *Health promotion & education research methods:*

Using the five chapter thesis/dissertation model (2nd ed.). Burlington, MA: Jones

and Bartlett Learning.

Creswell, J. W. (2009). *Research design: Qualitative, quantitative, and mixed methods*

approaches (3rd ed.). Thousand Oaks, CA: Sage.

Creswell, J. W. (2012). *Educational research: Planning, conducting, and evaluating*

quantitative and qualitative research (4th ed). Boston, MA: Pearson.

Creswell, J. W. & Plano Clark, V. L. (2011). *Designing and conducting mixed methods*

research (2nd ed.). Thousand Oaks, CA: Sage.

Dean, J., & Ghemawat, S. (2004, December). MapReduce: Simplified data processing on large clusters. *Proceedings of the 6th Symposium on Operating System Design and Implementation*, San Francisco, CA, 137-150. Retrieved from http://static.googleusercontent.com/external_content/untrusted_dlcp/research.google.com/en/us/archive/mapreduce-osdi04.pdf

Deshpande, T., Katsaros, P., Basagiannis, S., & Smolka, S. (2011, November). Formal analysis of the DNS bandwidth amplification attack and its countermeasures using probabilistic model checking. *Proceedings of the 2011 IEEE 2013 International Symposium on High-Assurance Systems Engineering*, Boca Raton, FL, 360-367. Retrieved from http://doi.ieeecomputersociety.org/10.1109/HASE.2011.57

Dittrich, D. (2012, April). So you want to take over a botnet. *Proceedings of the 5th USENIX Workshop on Large-Scale Exploits and Emergent Threats, LEET '12*, San Jose, CA. Retrieved from https://www.usenix.org/system/files/conference/leet12/leet12-final23.pdf

Doyal, A., Zhan, J., & Yu, H. (2012, December). Towards defeating distributed denial of service attacks. *Proceedings of the 2012 International Conference on Cyber Security*, Alexandria, VA, 209-212. Retrieved from http://doi.ieeecomputersociety.org/10.1109/CyberSecurity.2012.34

Erbarcher, R. & Shevenell, M. (2012). Design and implementation of an open network and host-based intrusion detection testbed with an emphasis on accuracy and repeatability. *Proceedings of the 2012 Ninth International Conference on Information Technology: New Generations*, Las Vegas, NV, 409-416. doi: doi:10.1109/ITNG.2012.99

Fachkha, C., Bou-Hard, E., & Debbabi, M. (2013, August). Towards a forecasting model for distributed denial of service activities. *Proceedings of the 2013 IEEE 12th International Symposium on Network Computing and Applications*, Cambridge, MA, 110-17. Retrieved from

http://doi.ieeecomputersociety.org/10.1109/NCA.2013.13

Fedynyshyn, G., Chuah, M., & Tan, G. (2011, September). Detection and classification of different botnet C&C channels. *Proceedings of the 8th International Conference on Autonomic and Trusted Computing*, Banff, Canada. Retrieved from http://www.cse.lehigh.edu/~gtan/paper/ATC2011.pdf

Feily, M., Shahrestani, A., & Ramadass, S. (2009, June). A survey of botnet and botnet detection. *Proceedings of the 2009 Third International Conference on Emerging Security Information, Systems and Technologies*, Athens, Glyfada, Greece, 268-273. Retrieved from

http://doi.ieeecomputersociety.org/10.1109/SECURWARE.2009.48

Francois, J., Wang, S., Bronzi, W., State, R., & Engel, T. (2011, November). BotCloud: Detecting botnets using Mapreduce. *Proceedings of the 2011 IEEE International Workshop on Information Forensics and Security*, Iguazu Falls, Parana, Brazil, 1-6. Retrieved from http://dx.doi.org/10.1109/WIFS.2011.6123125

Garant, D., & Lu, Wei. (2013). Mining botnet behaviors on the large-sale web application community. Proceedings of the *2013 27th International Conference on Advanced Information Networking and Applications Workshops*, Barcelona, Spain, 185-190. Retrieved from http://doi.ieeecomputersociety.org/10.1109/WAINA.2013.235

Garber, L. (2013). Security, privacy, policy, and dependability roundup. *IEEE Security and Privacy*, 11(4). 6-7. Retrieved from

    http://doi.ieeecomputersociety.org/10.1109/MSP.2013.97

Garfinkel, S. (2011, July 17). Network packet dumps. [Web log post]. Retrieved from

    http://digitalcorpora.org/corp/nps/scenarios/2009-m57-patents/net/

Greenhouse, S. W., & Geisser, S. (1959). On methods in the analysis of profile data. *Psychometrika, 24*, 95-112. Retrieved from:

    http://psycnet.apa.org/doi/10.1007/BF02289823

Geva, M., Herzberg, A., & Gez, Y. (2013, May). Bandwidth distributed denial of service: Attacks and defenses, *IEEE Security and Privacy, 11*(5). Retrieved from

    http://doi.ieeecomputersociety.org/10.1109/MSP.2013.55

Gu, G., Perdisci, R., Zhang, J., & Lee, W. (2008, July). BotMiner: Clustering analysis of network traffic for protocol and structure independent botnet detection. *Proceedings of the 17th USENEX Security Symposium,* San Jose, CA. Retrieved from https://www.usenix.org/legacy/event/sec08/tech/full_papers/gu/gu.pdf

Gu, G., Porras, P., Yegneswaran, V., Fong, M., & Lee, W. (2007, August). BotHunter: Detecting malware infection through IDS-driven dialog correlation. *Proceedings of the 16th USENEX Security Symposium,* Boston, MA. Retrieved from https://www.usenix.org/legacy/events/sec07/tech/full_papers/gu/gu.pdf

Gu, G., Yegneswaran, V., Porras, P., Stoll, J., & Lee, W. (2009, December). Active botnet probing to identify obscure command and control channels. *Proceedings of the 2009 Annual Computer Security Applications Conference,* Honolulu, HI, 241-253. doi: 10.1109/ACSAC.2009.30

Gu, G., Zhang, J., & Lee, W. (2008, February). BotSinffer: Detecting botnet command and control channels in network traffic. *Proceedings of the 15ᵗʰ Annual Network and Distributed System Security Symposium,* San Diego, CA. Retrieved from http://www.isoc.org/isoc/conferences/ndss/08/papers/17_botsniffer_ detecting_botnet.pdf

Hadoop (2013). The Apache Hadoop project. Retrieved from http://hadoop.apache.org/

Han, F., Chen, Z., Xu, H., & Liang, Y. (2012, June). Garlic: A distributed botnets suppression system. *Proceedings of the 2012 32ⁿᵈ International Conference on Distributed Computing Systems Workshops*, Macau, China, 634-639. Retrieved from http://doi.ieeecomputersociety.org/10.1109/ICDCSW.2012.30

Hasan, A., Awadi, R., & Belaton, B. (2013). Multi-phase IRC botnet and botnet behavior detection model. *International Journal of Computer Applications, 66*(15), 41-51. doi: 10.5120/11164-6289

Hayter, A. (2012). *Probability and statistics for engineers and scientists* (4ᵗʰ ed.). Boston, MA: Cengage.

Householder, A., & Danyliw, R. (2003, March). *Increased activity targeting windows shares* (CERT advisory CA-2003-08). Retrieved from http://www.cert.org/advisories/CA-2003-08.html

Hsu, D., & Marinucci, D. (2013). *Advances in cyber security*. New York, NY: Fordham University Press.

Hussain, A., Heidemann, J., & Papadopoulos, C. (2006). Identification of repeated denial of service attacks. *Proceedings of the 25ᵗʰ IEEE International Conference on*

Computer Communications, INFOCOM 2006, Barcelona, Spain, 1-15. Retrieved from http://dx.doi.org/10.1109/INFOCOM.2006.126

Ilavarasan, E. & Muthumanickam, K. (2012, July). Peer-to-peer botnet detection: combined host and network level analysis. *Proceedings of the Third International Conference on Computing Communications and Networking Technologies*, Coimbatore, India, 1-5. doi:10.1109/ICCCNT.2012.6395940

Jun, J., Oh, H., & Kim, S. (2011, December). Distributed denial of service flooding attack detection through a step-by-step investigation. *Proceedings of the 2011 IEEE 2nd International Conference on Networked Embedded Systems for Enterprise Applications*, Fremantle, WA. doi:10.1109/NESEA.2011.6144944

Karasaridis, A., Rexford, B., & Hoeflin, D. (2007, April). Wide-scale botnet detection and characterization. *Proceedings of the First Workshop on Hot Topics in Understanding Botnets*, Cambridge, MA. Retrieved from https://www.usenix.org/legacy/event/hotbots07/tech/full_papers/karasaridis/karas aridis.pdf

Khattak, R., Bano, S., Hussain, S., & Anwar, Z. (2011, December). Dofur: Distributed denial of service forensics using Mapreduce. *Proceedings of the 2011 Frontiers of Information Technology Conference*, Islamabad, Pakistan. doi: 10.1109/FIT.2011.29

Kline, E., Beaumont-Gay, M., Mirkovic, J., & Reiher, P. (2009, December). Rad: Reflector attack defense using message authentication codes. *Proceedings of the 2009 Annual Computer Security Applications Conference*, Honolulu, HI, 269-278. Retrieved from http://doi.ieeecomputersociety.org/10.1109/ACSAC.2009.32

Kumar, A., Chandak, S., & Dewanjee, R. (2014). Recent advances in intrusion detection systems: An analytical evaluation and comparative study. *International Journal of Computer Applications, 86*(4), 32-37. doi: 10.5120/14975-3172

Leder, F., Werner, R., & Martini, P. (2009, June). Proactive botnet countermeasures an offensive approach. *Proceedings of the Conference on Cyber Warfare 2009,* Tallinn, Estonia. Retrieved from http://www.ccdcoe.org/publications/virtualbattlefield/15_LEDER_Proactive_Cout nermeasures.pdf

Lee, J., Kwon, J., Shin, H., & Lee, H. (2010, October). Tracking multiple C&C botnets by analyzing DNS traffic. *Proceedings of the 2010 6th IEEE Workshop on Secure Network Protocols*, Kyoto, Japan, 67-72. Retrieved from http://dx.doi.org/10.1109/NPSEC.2010.5634445

Leedy, P., & Ormrod, J. (2012). Practical *research: Planning and design* (10th ed.). Boston, MA: Pearson.

Li, Q., Larsen, C., & Van der Horst, T. (2013). IPv6: A catalyst and evasion tool for botnets and malware delivery networks. *Computer, 46*(5), 76-82. Retrieved from http://doi.ieeecomputersociety.org/10.1109/MC.2012.296

Li, W., Xie, S., Luo, J., & Zhu, X. (2013, April). A detection method for botnet based on behavior features. *Proceedings of the 2nd International Conference on Systems Engineering and Modeling (ICSEM-13)*, Beijing, China, 512-517. Retrieved from http://www.atlantis-press.com/php/download_paper.php?id=5594

Liao, M., Li, J., Yang, C., Chen, M., Tsai, C., & Change, M. (2012, July). Botnet topology reconstruction: A case study. *Proceedings of the 2012 Sixth*

International Conference on Innovative Mobile and Internet Services in

   Ubiquitous Computing, Palermo, Italy, 529-534. Retrieved from

   http://doi.ieeecomputersociety.org/10.1109/IMIS.2012.114

Lincoln Laboratory. (2014). DARPA intrusion detection data sets. Retrieved from

   http://www.ll.mit.edu/mission/communications/cyber/CSTcorpora/ideval/data/ind

   ex.html

Lu, C., & Brooks, R. (2013). Timing analysis in P2P botnet traffic using probabilistic

   context-free grammars. *Proceedings of the Eighth Annual Cyber Security and*

   Information Intelligence Research Workshop (CSIIRW '13), New York, NY, 1-4.

   Retrieved from http://dx.doi.org/10.1145/2459976.2459992

Meenakshi, S., Raghavan, S., & Bhaskar, S. (2011, October). A study on path behavior

   characteristics of IPv6 based reflector attacks. *Proceedings of the 2011 IEEE 36th*

   Conference on Local Computer Networks, Bonn, Germany, 927-933. Retrieved

   from http://doi.ieeecomputersociety.org/10.1109/LCN.2011.6115573

Nagaraja, S., Mittal, P., Hong, C., Caesar, M., and Borisov, N. (2010, August). BotGrep:

   Finding P2P bots with structured graph analysis. *Proceedings of the 19th USENIX*

   Security Symposium, Washington, DC. Retrieved from

   https://www.usenix.org/legacy/event/sec10/tech/full_papers/Nagaraja.pdf

NS-2 (2009). The Network Simulator (Version 2) [Computer Software]. Los Angeles,

   CA: Author. Available from http://www.isi.edu/nsnam/ns/index.html

Oikarinen, J., & Reed, D. (1993). Internet relay chat protocol RFC 1459. *Internet*

   Engineering Task Force. Retrieved from

   http://http://tools.ietf.org/html/rfc1459.html

P, V., Laxmi, V., & Gaur, M. (2009, March). Survey on malware detection methods. *Proceedings of the 3rd Hackers' Workshop on Computer and Internet Security*, Kanpur, India. Retrieved from http://www.security.iitk.ac.in/contents/events/workshops/iitkhack09/papers/vinod.pdf

Paxton, N., Ahn, G., & Shehab, M. (2011, July). MasterBlaster: Identifying influential players in botnet transactions. *Proceedings of the 35th Annual Computer Software and Applications Conference*, Munich, Germany, 413-419. doi:10.1109/COMPSAC.2011.61

Raghava, N., Sahgal, D., & Chandna, S. (2012). Classification of botnet detection based on botnet architecture. *Proceedings of the 2012 International Conference on Communication Systems and Network Topologies,* Rajkot, India, 569-572. Retrieved from http://doi.ieeecomputersociety.org/10.1109/CSNT.2012.128

Roscini, M. (2014). *Cyber operations and the use of force in international law*. New York, NY: Oxford University Press

Rossow, C., Andriesse, D., Werner, T., Stone-Gross, B., Plohmann, D., Dietrich, C., & Bos, H. (2013, May). SoK: peer-to-peerwned – modeling and evaluating the resilience of peer-to-peer botnets. *Proceedings of the 2013 IEEE Symposium on Security and Privacy*, Berkeley, CA, 97-111. Retrieved from http://doi.ieeecomputersociety.org/10.1109/SP.2013.17

Rossow, C., & Dietrich, C. (2013, July). PROVEX: Detecting botnets with encrypted command and control channels. *Proceedings of the 10th International Conference on Detection of Intrusions and Malware, and Vulnerability Assessment,* Berlin,

Heidelberg, 21-40. Retrieved from http://dx.doi.org/10.1007/978-3-642-39235-
1_2

Salkind, N. J. (2012). *Exploring research* (8th ed.). Boston, MA: Pearson.

Scarfone, K., & Mell, P. (2012). *Guide to intrusion detection and prevention systems
IPDS draft* (NIST Special Publication 800-94 Revision 1 Draft). Retrieved from
http://csrc.nist.gov/publications/drafts/800-94-rev1/draft_sp800-94-rev1.pdf

Shah, C. (2011, February). *Evolving ddos botnets: 1. blackenergy*. Retrieved from
McAfee Labs Website: http://blogs.mcafee.com/business/security-
connected/evolving-ddos-botnets-1-blackenergy

Snieder, R., & Larner, K. (2009). *The art of being a scientist: A guide for graduate
students and their mentors*. New York: Cambridge University Press.

Spitzner, L. (2003). The honeynet project: Trapping the hackers. *IEEE Security &
Privacy, 1*(2), 15-23. doi: 10.1109/MSECP.2003.1193207

Tao, Y., & Yu, S. (2013, July). DDoS attack detection at local area networks using
information theoretical metrics. *Proceedings of the 2013 12th IEEE International
Conference on Trust, Security, and Privacy in Computing and Communications*,
Melbourne, Australia, 233-240. Retrieved from
http://doi.ieeecomputersociety.org/10.1109/TrustCom.2013.32

Trost, R. (2010). *Practical intrusion detection*. Boston, MA: Pearson.

Tsai, C., Chang, A., & Ming-Szu, H. (2010, October). Early warning system for DDoS
attacking based on multilayer deployment of time delay neural network.
Proceedings of the 2010 Sixth International Conference on Intelligent

Information Hdiing and Multimedia Signal Processing (IIH-MSP), Darmstadt, Germany, 704-707. Retrieved from http://dx.doi.org/10.1109/IIHMSP.2010.178

Ventre, D. (2013). *Cyber Conflict: Competing National Perspectives*. Indianapolis, IN: Wiley.

Wang, P., Sparks, S., & Zou, C. C. (2010). An advanced hybrid peer-to-peer botnet. *IEEE Transactions on Dependable and Secure Computing, 7*(2), 113-127. doi:10.1109/TDSC.2008.35

Wang, T., Wang, H., & Shi, P. (2013). What is the pattern of a botnet? *Proceedings of the 2013 12th IEEE International Conference on Trust, Security and Privacy in Computing and Communications*, Melbourne, Australia, 257-264. Retrieved from http://doi.ieeecomputersociety.org/10.1109/TrustCom.2013.35

Wang, T., & Yu, S. (2009). Centralized botnet detection by traffic aggregation. *Proceedings of the 2009 IEEE International Symposium on Parallel and Distributed Processing with Applications*, Chengdu, China, 86-93. Retrieved from http://dx.doi.org/10.1109/ISPA.2009.74

Ward, L. (2009, April 10). Openpacket.org – example.com PCAP files. [Web log post]. Retrieved from http://leonward.wordpress.com/2009/04/10/openpacketorg-examplecom-pcap-files/

Weimer, W., Fry, Z., & Forrest, S. (2013, November). Leveraging program equivalence for adaptive program repair: Models and first results. *Proceedings of the 2013 IEEE/ACM 28th International Conference on Automated Software Engineering*, Silicon Valley, CA, 356-366. Retrieved from http://dx.doi.org/10.1109/ASE.2013.6693094

Whitman, W., & Mattord, H. (2012). *Principles of information security* (4th ed.). Boston, MA: Cengage.

Wireshark Foundation. (2014). Wireshark (Version 1.10.8) [Computer Software]. Retrieved from http://www.wireshark.org/download.html

Woods, K., Lee, C., Garfinkel, S., Dittrich, D., Rusell, A., & Kearton, K. (2011). Creating realistic corpora for security and forensic education. *Proceedings of the ADFSL Conference on Digital Forensics, Secuirty, and Law, 2011*, Richmond, VA, 123-134. Retrieved from http://www.dtic.mil/cgi-bin/GetTRDoc?AD=ADA549432

Xiang, C., Binxing, F., Peng, L., & Chaoge, L. (2012). Advanced triple channel botnets: model and implementation. *Proceedings of the 2012 ACM Conference on Computer and Communications Security*, Raleigh, NC, 1019-1021. Retrieved from http://dx.doi.org/10.1145/2382196.2382311

Yang, J., Park, M., & Chung, T. (2013). A study of low-rate DDoS attacks in real networks. *Proceedings of the 2013 International Conference on Information Science and Applications*, Suwon, Korea, 1-4. Retrieved from http://doi.ieeecomputersociety.org/10.1109/ICISA.2013.6579418

Yong, W., Tefera, S., & Beshah, Y. (2012, August). Understanding botnet: From modelling to integrated detection and mitigation framework. *Proceedings of the 2012 13th ACIS International Conference on Software Engineering, Artificial Intelligence, Networking and Parallel/Distributed Computing*, Kyoto, Japan, 63-70. Retrieved from http://doi.ieeecomputersociety.org/10.1109/SNPD.2012.78

Yi, F., Yu, S., Zhou, W., Hai, J., & Bonti, A. (2008). Source-based filtering scheme against distributed denial of service attacks. *International Journal of Database Theory and Application, 1*(1), 9-20. Retrieved from http://hdl.handle.net/10536/DRO/DU:30017709

Yu, S., James, S., Tian, Y, & Dou, W. (2012). Reliable aggregation on network traffic for web based knowledge discovery. In H. Dai, J. Liu & E. Smirnov (Eds.), *Reliable Knowledge Discovery* (pp. 149-159). doi: 10.1007/978-1-4614-1903-7_8

Zargar, S., Joshi, J., & Tipper, D. (2013). A survey of defense mechanisms against distributed denial of service (distributed denial of service) flooding attacks. *IEEE Communications Surveys and Tutorials, PP*(99), 1-24. doi: 10.1109/SURV.2013.031413.00127

Zeng, Y. (2012). *On detection of current and next-generation botnets* (Doctoral dissertation). University of Michigan. Retrieved from http://deepblue.lib.umich.edu/handle/2027.42/91382

Zeng, Y., Hu, X., & Shin, K. (2010, June). Detection of botnets using combined host and network level information. *Proceedings of the 2010 IEEE/IFIP International Conference on Dependable Systems and Networks*, Chicago, IL, 291-300. Retrieved from http://doi.ieeecomputersociety.org/10.1109/DSN.2010.5544306

Zhang, J. (2012). *Effective and scalable botnet detection in network traffic.* (Doctoral Dissertation). Retrieved from ProQuest Dissertations and Theses database. (AAT 1115317916)

Zhang, J., Perdisci, R., Lee, W., Sarfraz, U., & Luo, X. (2011, June). Detecting stealthy P2P botnets using statistical traffic fingerprints. *Proceedings of the 2011*

IEEE/IFIP 41st International Conference on Dependable Systems and Networks, Hong Kong, China, 121-132. Retrieved from http://doi.ieeecomputersociety.org/10.1109/DSN.2011.5958212

Zhuge, J., Holz, T., Han, X., Guo, J., & Zou, W. (2007, December). *Characterizing the IRC-Based Botnet Phenomenon.* Peking University and University of Mannheim Technical Report. Retrieved from https://ub-madoc.bib.uni-mannheim.de/1710/1/botnet_china_TR.pdf

APPENDIX A – COMPUTER CONFIGURATION

Dell Precision 6600

Intel Core ™ i7 2920X CPU @ 2.50GHz

16GB RAM

Ubuntu 12.04 64-bit Operating System

APPENDIX B – LEON WARD EMAIL

Date:	Sun, 9 Feb 2014 22:05:04 +0000 [02/09/14 17:05:04 EST]
From:	"Leon Ward (leonward)" <leonward@cisco.com>
To:	"tshyslip@capitol-college.edu" <tshyslip@capitol-college.edu>
Cc:	"leon.ward@sourcefire.com" <leon.ward@sourcefire.com>
Subject:	Re: Example.com pcaps
Headers:	Show All Headers

Go for it.

Yes the last one or two contain some malicious activity.

Sent from a mobile device. Apologies for any typos but they happen.

[Hide Quoted Text]
> On 9 Feb 2014, at 20:56, "tshyslip@capitol-college.edu"
<tshyslip@capitol-college.edu> wrote:
>
> Leon,
>
> Hello, my name is Tom Hyslip. I am a graduate student at Capitol
College working on my Doctor of Science degree. I found your Wordpress
blog with the example.com pcaps. I am writing to ask you permission to
use the pcaps in my research. I would use the pcaps to mimic normal
Internet activity for testing an IDS for false positives. Of course, if
you approve I would cite and reference your work as the source of the
pcaps.
>
> One question about the pcaps, your comments on the blog say
example.com-1.pcap through example.com-8-overnight.pcap do not contain
any intentional malicious traffic, but later captures do. Would that be
example.com-9-addition-of-rouge-1.pcap and example.com-9-addition-of-
rouge-2.pcap? I just want to verify which pcaps contain malicious
activity. Finally, if you approve, I would like to use your picture
file showing the test network as a reference to your pcaps. Thank you
very much for your time, I look forward to hearing from you. And thank
you for taking time to provide these pcaps, it is very difficult to
find pcaps to use in research experiments.
>
> Yours truly,
> Tom Hyslip

APPENDIX C – DIGITAL CORPORA

Home

February 22nd, 2011

DigitalCorpora.org is a website of digital corpora for use in computer forensics education research. All of the disk images, memory dumps, and network packet captures available on this website are freely available and may be used without prior authorization or IRB approval. We also have available a research corpus of real data acquired from around the world. Use of that dataset is possible under special arrangement.

From here you can view the available:

- Cell Phone Dumps
- Disk Images
- Files
- Network Packet Dumps
- Scenarios

Many of the corpora are distributed in RAW, EnCase E01, and Advanced Forensic Format (AFF) formats. We also make available a Digital Forensics XML file for many of the disk images that describes the files contained within each volume. You can download tools for working with AFF and XFXML files from our companion website, http://afflib.org/.

Publications describing these corpora and our related research can be found on our publications page.

APPENDIX D – LITERATURE SEARCH

Key Word Search	Peer Reviewed Works Reviewed	Germinal Works Reviewed	Books Reviewed	Studies Reviewed
Botnet	42	17	7	5
Botnet Detection	35	13	2	3
Botnet Identification	8	6	0	0
Proactive Botnet	3	7	0	0
Distributed Denial of Service	31	15	5	4
Denial of Service	11	7	2	1
Malware	17	16	3	3
Experimental Research	11	4	5	0
Encrypted Botnet	12	7	0	3
Honeypot	9	5	1	0
Snort	14	7	2	3
Egress filtering	4	4	1	0
Statistics	0	2	1	0
Total Documents Reviewed (358)	197	110	29	22

APPENDIX E: METHODOLOGY MAP

Quantitative Quasi Experimental Study Research
- Botnet and Distributed Denial of Service attack evaluation
- Contribute to knowledge of information assurance and incident response fields

Pilot Study

- To aid in ensuring validity and reliability of study
- Test experimental instrument with known DDoS packets and non-malicious traffic
- Analyze Snort alerts to ensure 100% true detection and 0% true negative
- Adjust Snort alerts if results are less than 100% detection and 0% true negative

Primary Data Collection

- Experimental procedure with fifteen (15) sample populations
- Test each sample population against eight Snort rules developed from 4 independent variables and record number of false positive alerts (dependent variable)
- Test two known DDoS packet captures against eight Snort rules and record number of true positive alerts

Data Analysis

- Transcribe Snort alerts to Excel Spreadsheet
- Complete Data Collection, Transcription, Coding
- Constantly compare Data
- Calculate Descriptive statistics with Excel
    - Mean, Mode, Median, Range, Standard Deviation, Variance
    - False positive rate, true positive rate
- Calculate Inferential Statistics Excel
    - Repeated Measures ANOVA, alpha = 0.1
    - Paired t-test for each set of independent variables, alpha = 0.1
- Finalize Data Interpretations

Interpret Data and Report Results

- Interpret Data Analysis results
- Reject Null Hypothesis if
    - Repeated Measures ANOVA: $F > F$ critical
    - Paired t-test: $p < 0.1$
- Assess Effectiveness of Approach in Comparison to Past Research
- Compile Evaluation Report for Study Organization
- Submit Final Dissertation paper to Capitol College

www.ingramcontent.com/pod-product-compliance
Lightning Source LLC
LaVergne TN
LVHW060144070326
832902LV00018B/2947